MW00676694

"THERE IS NO RANDOMNESS ABOUT YOUR LIFE"

A Journey of Faith, Hope, Love and Strength

By

Libby Teston Auers

"THERE IS NO RANDOMNESS ABOUT YOUR LIFE"

A Journey of Faith, Hope, Love and Strength

©2016 Libby Teston Auers

All Rights Reserved

All rights reserved in all media. No part of this book may be used or reproduced without written permission of the Author and the Publisher.

First Publication

Published in the United States of America
Published by
ATC Publishing
P.O. Box 714
Sharpsburg, GA 30277

ISBN-13: 978-0-9910913-6-2
ISBN-10: 0-9910913-6-1

Devotionals taken from 'Jesus Calling' by Sarah Young - Copyright © 2004 by Sarah Young are used by permission of Thomas Nelson. www.thomas nelson.com

DEDICATION

To my precious husband Loren,
You have loved me and cared for me for
more than
Half my life,
You encouraged me always
And still do.
Thank you for showing me what
It means to believe in HIM at all times,
And in all things,
But most of all,
Thank you for spending
The rest of your life with me.
I will love you and carry you within my
heart... Forever.

FORWARD

By Erin M. Dunbar, M.D.
Neuro-Oncology
Piedmont Brain Tumor Center

Loren's unique combination of perseverance, courage, grace and humor was truly one of a kind. Everyone on my team and everyone in the hospital always commented on how he and his wife made them smile from deep within their hearts. Loren effortlessly provided us the emotional rewards we all hoped our vocations in healthcare would bring us. It was a phenomenal privilege to have cared for him...and to have known his family.

Loren reminds me fondly of one of my favorite secular quotes describing the intimate and beautiful intertwining of human relationships, paraphrased as "because in life we are all walking each-other home."

Everyone who had the privilege of knowing Loren enjoyed unparalleled beauty in that walk. Loren lived his life as the embodiment of the Christian prayer of St. Francis of Assisi. He made the world a phenomenally better place for us all as we continue helping each-other in the service of "walking each-other home."

It brings me joy to know that each of us will take the wisdom we learned from Loren on with us.

Dr. Erin Dunbar

ACKNOWLEDGEMENTS

First, and most importantly, I want to thank our Heavenly Father. Without a shadow of a doubt it was HIS unending love that carried us throughout the year of Loren's illness. HE helped us understand that with that love fear would only be momentary if we continued to trust HIM and HIS promise to us all...Eternal Life.

I want to thank my extraordinary husband Loren. Each day before I would post my journaling I would read it to him. He would look at me, smile and say, "Beautiful Hummies, post it." And when someone would respond to the posts and say, "Libby you need to put these posts in a book," he would nod his head and say, "Yes, you need to put these in a book." And so it is. He encouraged me then, and he continues to encourage me now. His love lives on in my heart and my soul and my life has been blessed immeasurably because of the gift of that love.

My heartfelt thanks to Dr. Erin Dunbar for her beautiful remembrance of Loren which she shared in the forward of this book. I also want to thank her for her wisdom and encouragement in "keeping a journal" while we walked the nearly yearlong journey through Loren's illness. We did not know where the journey would take us, but as she so beautifully reminds us in the forward, "we are all just walking each-other home." This book, the journey of what seemed like a million miles, would not have happened were it not for the words she shared with us on the first day she met with us in April of 2014.

I would also like to extend my gratitude to author Sarah Young and her publisher Thomas Nelson for granting permission for the use of quotes from her daily devotional Jesus Calling. Loren and I were given a copy of Jesus Calling just weeks after his diagnosis. We found strength and solace in its words each day and when I recall the many beautiful conversations that Loren and I would have after spending time reading its words my heart is full of peace and joy. So often after our conversations I would be inspired to sit and share our thoughts, our hopes and our prayers through my writing.

INTRODUCTION

Saturday, April 19th, 2014 was the beginning of a journey that none of us wants to take. Loren my husband, who I had been married to for 33 years, had not been feeling well for several months. He had been to the doctor numerous times and the only outcome of the bloodwork that was drawn over and over again was "low testosterone". Loren was 58 years old at the time and had always been in extremely good health.

My concerns continued to grow as I had seen many drastic changes in Loren, both physically and mentally. Needless to say, I was not in agreement with Loren's doctor. After a long discussion the three of us did agree to give testosterone replacement a try, but after several days on the medication his symptoms continued to worsen.

Loren began obsessing over things he had or had not done as well as having difficulty with his short-term memory and he was becoming weaker by the day. On Friday night one of the more frightening things happened. He had gone up to take his bath. As I sat downstairs I had the most sickening feeling that something was wrong and that I should go to check on him. My instincts were right. When I reached the doorway of our bedroom the upper part of his body was sprawled across the bed while his lower half hung off the foot of the bed. He was naked and the lower half of his body was horribly red. I rushed into the room saying, "Dear God honey, what did you do?" He turned his head, looked up at me and said, "I guess I got the water too hot. I couldn't remember how to work the faucet." I was horrified. I knew in that moment that there was so much more to this than "low testosterone."

I barely slept that night. I laid awake sick to my stomach and fought back tears throughout the night. At six o'clock on the morning of April 19th I got up out of bed, went downstairs, and called our oldest son on FaceTime. As soon as I saw his face I began to cry. I told him how scared I was about his father and that I knew what was happening was far more serious than "low testosterone." He suggested that I take him to the emergency room. It's not as if that had not occurred to me, but I was afraid Loren would fight me about going there. After all, he had been going to the doctor for months.

Encouraged by Loren's neuro-oncologist, what follows is the nearly yearlong journey. For Loren and for me it was a journey of discovering so many things about ourselves, as individuals, but also about our love and commitment to one another. It was a journey that was filled with faith and hope and strength. Throughout the entire journey it was always about Loren's love for God, his love for me and his love for his family. Selfless. There is no other way to describe this man. This beautiful man who I had the privilege of calling my husband for thirty-four years.

I am thankful to the many people who would read my daily journaling and encouraged me to put them here in this book.

I pray that when you read these words, at times full of pain and fear, but many more of hope and strength, that you realize the things that you may be experiencing in your own life have purpose, and that there is "no randomness" in our journeys. I hope that these words help you to remember that God has a journey, a plan, for each of us. It may not be a path of our choosing, but there will be many lessons and blessings along the way. I pray that you find faith, hope, love and strength along your journey, whatever that journey may be.

Our Journey Begins

APRIL - 2014

April 19, 2014

~ Holy Saturday. Our daughter-in-law was coming with our grandson to spend the day, and some of our family is going to be spending Easter Sunday together. I had not had the opportunity to grocery shop. The grocery store became somewhere I did not like to go with Loren any longer. He had walked away from me several times in the store in the past few weeks and I would find him wandering around aimlessly, much like an Alzheimer patient might. I needed to grocery shop however. My plan was to brush my teeth, throw my clothes on and get to the grocery store and back before Loren was out of bed, but it didn't exactly happen like that. By the time I was finished in the bathroom Loren was awake and wanting to eat breakfast. He said he was going to go downstairs and fix himself some cereal. I went down a short while later and found his bowl of cereal sitting on the kitchen counter with the milk carton next to it. The milk was poured, but Loren was downstairs sitting in his recliner with a blanket across his lap watching ESPN. I looked at him from the top of stairs that led to our family room and fought back tears. I asked, "Honey, are you going to eat your cereal?" He turned and looked at me and said, "I already did." I reminded him that his cereal was on the kitchen counter and to come up and eat it. I sat with him while he did. When he was finished he went back to his recliner and I made him promise me that he would stay there until I came home. I grocery shopped faster than I had in my entire life.

When I returned home Loren came out to help unload the groceries from the car and he helped to put them away in the kitchen. In the weeks leading up to this day he had not been eating very well. He would pack his lunch for work (yes, he worked right up until his diagnosis) but he would bring half of his lunch home with him in the afternoon. Sitting on the counter from his lunch the day before was an orange that he had not eaten. I was washing a couple of things out in the sink. I picked up the orange and handed it to him asking him if he would put it in the refrigerator for me. The refrigerator was behind me and I could sense him hesitating. I was afraid to turn around, but I did. Next to the refrigerator is a small cabinet where we keep our toaster and some other odds and ends. Loren was standing there with the cabinet door open holding the orange. He just stared at the orange in his hand. I asked him, "Honey, what are you doing?" He said, "I'm putting the orange away." Then I asked him where he was putting it. "In the refrigerator." Dear God in Heaven! I said, "Honey, the refrigerator is right next to you, the big silver thing." "Oh." I wanted to turn around and vomit into the kitchen sink. At that moment I knew that what was happening to Loren was going to change our lives forever.

Our daughter-in-law arrived at our house a short time later with our grandson. Loren went downstairs with our grandson and I shared the events of the past twenty-four hours with her. What I saw that morning when we walked down the stairs to where Loren and our

2

grandson were broke my heart, and still does when I think about it today. Loren was sitting on the rug with his legs tucked underneath him and our little grandson had climbed onto his lap and had his arms around Loren's neck. I am convinced that he knew that his Papa was ill. He adored his Papa and his Papa adored him. It was a tender moment. One I won't ever forget. We spoke to Loren about going to the hospital and it took us no time at all to convince him that we should go. When we arrived there and I explained to the woman at the desk what Loren's symptoms were, we were immediately taken back to an exam room. In less than fifteen minutes Loren was taken for a CT scan, and in less than a half an hour the ER doctor came to our room.

After several months of doctor visits it took less than an hour to hear the news that would change our lives forever. The CT scan showed a mass on Loren's brain. My husband had brain cancer. Loren was sleeping when the doctor came in. She looked over at him and rolled a stool around to where I was sitting. Before she even opened her mouth I knew what she would say. When she told me I sat there not uttering a word. It did not surprise me to hear those words. She asked if I was alright. How do you answer that question? "No. You just told me that my husband of 33 years has a mass on his brain." Loren woke up and the doctor repeated the news to him. He laid there listening to all of the "facts" as they knew them. They had already contacted the brain cancer center at Piedmont hospital in Atlanta, and Loren would be transported there as soon as possible.

It was Easter weekend. The most incredible miracle there ever was, THE resurrection of our Lord Jesus was to be celebrated the next day. Would Loren be a miracle? Would God in all HIS majesty grant us a miracle and bring Loren back to complete health? It was much too early to go there.

There was much to do. I had to call our four children. Our oldest son and his wife were on an Easter egg hunt with their little girl when I called. It is funny how the news we had just received was one of the most horrendous things one could hear, but I was so sorry that I had interrupted their Easter egg hunt. A half an hour later I received a phone call from him. He was in his car on his way to Georgia. Our second son lives nearby. Just a month or so before Loren's diagnosis he sat at our kitchen table and shared his concerns about his father. In fact, Loren's emotional and mental health had changed so much that his words were, "Mom, I think Dad is checking out." Such a heart wrenching memory for me now. He immediately came to the hospital and helped arrange transport to Atlanta as he works with our local fire department. Our third son lives just north of Atlanta and also came quickly to the hospital. The last phone call I made was to our daughter. She is our youngest child and our only daughter. She adores her father. Dear God, this is the phone call I least wanted to make and the one that is etched into my memory. I will never forget hearing her cry of despair as I shared the news with her. She and her husband are serving in the military and she was on temporary duty away from her husband and all things familiar to her. My biggest regret is that I did not call her husband first so that I could let him know that she was so desperately going to need him. My last words to her were "call your husband". She immediately made arrangements to fly home so that they would come to Atlanta together.

One of the first phone calls I made after I called our children was to our longtime friend and Pastor, Father John. He came immediately to the hospital. He anointed Loren and when he did Loren began to cry. He asked Loren what he most feared at that moment. The answer he gave in that moment he repeated time and again throughout the yearlong journey. He said, "I am afraid of leaving Libby alone. I just want her to be okay."

After being transported to Atlanta Loren was placed under the care of neuro-oncologist Dr. Erin Dunbar. She is a brilliant doctor, but more importantly she is a woman of deep faith. That was so evident in our first meeting with her, and so very important to us. She knows that she is but an instrument of God, and that her talent and knowledge is all a gift from HIM.

April 22, 2014

~ To our dear family and friends, words cannot express the gratitude Loren and I have in our hearts for prayers that are lifting us up during this time. Please know that we truly FEEL them and they are keeping Loren's, mine and our children's hearts full. We know that through your love and prayers and THE ONE who can work miracles that we will be made strong through all of this. Please know that we are receiving ALL of your messages of love and support and that we love you all in return, even if we do not have the chance to respond to each one of you individually. God Bless all of you!

Today Loren underwent a brain biopsy. We have learned the preliminary results of the biopsy with a full report to come later. Loren has lymphoma. We will know more after further testing, but Loren's doctor is extremely positive. We will pray, we will believe, we will walk this journey.

April 23, 2014

~ It has been a difficult day for Loren. The brain biopsy surgery is making him feel ill and he, as you might imagine, has had a headache all day. Dr. Dunbar wants to begin chemotherapy immediately. The cancer is aggressive and they want to stop the progression. There is no waiting. Regardless of how Loren is feeling the chemotherapy will begin tomorrow. I find it interesting that there has not really been a discussion as to whether or not Loren WANTS to have treatment. Not between Loren and me or between the doctor and Loren. Unspoken words. Maybe we just don't want to. Maybe the doctor just assumes that there is no doubt that Loren would want to do this. Loren did not say "no". It is his choice and his unspoken words tell me "yes". He wants to do this. I will stand beside him.

April 24, 2014

~ A new day on what looks to be a very long journey. I wanted to take a moment at the end of this day to say thank you to every single one of you who continues to pray for Loren, for me, and for our family. Tonight I am thankful to God for sending to us HIS instruments to be used in Loren's battle. Beautiful nurses who are full of compassion for not just their patient, but for our family. I am thankful for Loren's work family who unceasingly has let him and our family know how special and important he is to them. Feeling "special" and knowing you matter in others' lives gives you purpose and hope, and Loren is feeling that. He also feels the prayers that are being lifted to our Heavenly Father on his behalf.

We were greatly encouraged by news we received from the oncologist today. She is quite a cheerleader! She has the most calming and assuring demeanor, and she gives us much confidence that Loren will come through this battle. This will be a very long fight. Please know that your requests of "please let me help" will be granted. I ask for your continued prayers for Loren and your tireless support for me and for my children. We love you all and as we thank God for HIS love, we also thank you and will offer up prayers of thanksgiving to our Father for you. God bless you.

It is late evening and the nursing staff is preparing Loren for his first chemo treatment. We have waited all day for it to begin...all in HIS timing. We have tried to not allow our fear and anxiety take over throughout this long day.

*****

~ In a short while Loren's caregivers, the instruments of healing from our Heavenly Father, will begin the first of probably a year or more of chemo treatments. I thank our Father for blessing us with the extraordinary people He will have walking this journey along with us. Most of all I am thankful for the beautiful family that He gave us in our life together. They have been Loren's reason for knowing that he will give this battle EVERYTHING he has, and they have been my rock in these last few days. I ask that you pray for them, that they are strengthened by The Holy Spirit, that the Spirit fills them with peace and comfort along this journey. Thank you my family and friends, we love you all!

~ The journey begins...pray unceasingly.

April 25, 2014

~ It is 4AM....it's been a rough few hours...two large bags of what is supposed to be "the cure"... so how is it that it makes you feel so bad? Loren says, "This is the part I was dreading the most." He's being a trooper though. I ask you our friends for prayers of comfort for Loren. Love to you all.

*****

~ Our family gives Loren the courage to win...and the outstretched arms of Jesus on the cross will give him the strength that he will need. Thank you Jesus!

*****

Psalm 126:3
"The Lord has done great things for us, and we are filled with joy!"

~ The Lord has done GREAT things for us, and we are filled with JOY? I am imagining some of you may be thinking, "Really? How can she be thinking that? She must be full of denial!" No, not really. When I think about all that has transpired in this past week, one week ago tomorrow, I think about the many blessings that occurred that day. The promptings of our children who led me to believe that my gut feelings should be listened to. My daughter-in-law who came to our home late in the morning on Saturday and looked at Loren and said, "Yes, your gut is right, you MUST take him to the ER." The blessing of the incredibly compassionate ER doctor who brought the news that rocked our souls but was there to comfort and support us. And the talented doctors whose care we were placed into once brought to Atlanta. Yes, HE has done GREAT things and we are FILLED WITH JOY that HE loves and cares for us enough to have brought all of these people into our lives. The first stage of the first chemo treatment has been completed...two more to go in this first round. Continued prayers for Loren for his comfort, for his peace, and for his spirit to be filled with the JOY of the GREAT things the LORD has done! Love to you all!

*****

~ Prayers of Thanksgiving for the two nurses who have walked with Loren through this night. One is a lovely young lady who is compassionate and has definitely chosen the right vocation for her life. She is a beautiful servant and instrument of healing sent from God. The other is a veteran. (She is Loren's twin; they share the same exact birthdate, year and all) Care and devotion are two of her gifts. She also has the gift of experience and knowledge. She has answered every question as this first night has progressed. A difficult night, but we are blessed to have two wonderful ladies joining the journey. Praising God for them!

*****

~ The start of a new day...today we are giving thanks for our "Delta Family". On May 11th Loren will be a part of Delta Air Lines for thirty-three years, but never have we known what being a part of that "family" has meant until now. We will NEVER be able to express the gratitude we have in our hearts for the many visits, phone calls, texts, unbelievable generosity and most of all PRAYERS that they have continued to share since learning of Loren's illness last weekend. And we have learned since, that there were so many of his "brothers" who were working side by side with him who were sharing their concerns of him with one another. True "brothers" who I know will go above and beyond for him throughout this journey. We are sending our love to each and every one of them for their non-stop support. God Bless!

April 26, 2014

Deuteronomy 31:6
"Be strong and of good courage, do not fear nor be afraid of them; for the Lord your God, HE is the ONE who goes with you. He will not leave you nor forsake you."

~ This is my Loren. During the night he began stage three of his first round of chemo. He is feeling the effects of it this morning. Please send up prayers to uplift his spirit, that our Lord removes his discouragement and give him strength...with his heart full of love and soul full of good wishes from family and friends he is stepping out into this journey side by side with his Heavenly Father full of courage. With gratitude to you all!

"He will raise you up on eagle's wings, bear you on the breath of dawn, make you to shine like the sun, and hold you in the palm of HIS hand." ~ Michael Joncas

~ The words to this song have been repeating in my head throughout this day. I KNOW that God has Loren within the palm of his hand. The KNOWING and the HOLDING it in your heart can sometimes be hard to combine. Praying always that our faith sustains us through this time and as always, being full of gratitude for our loving family and friends who continue to lift us up in prayer.

* * * *

~ When darkness falls it is the toughest of times...pray without ceasing...

April 27, 2014

~ We will continue to ask for prayers and we thank you all for walking down this path with us. We felt your prayers throughout the night and a rough day was transformed into a better night. Loren received yet another type of chemo medication that could have come with other complications but PRAISE GOD he came through it like a champ according to his nurse. Another wonderful, extremely knowledgeable nurse who squelched every fear and anxiety that both Loren and I might have had throughout the night and made sure Loren was as comfortable as possible and he was able to get much needed rest. Continue to pray for his strength, both physically and spiritually as this morning he is expressing thoughts of "so, if I didn't get this treated..." We must keep him strong...as always I am grateful for all of you in our lives. God Bless!

*****

~ Today it is Sunday and I am missing my church "family" for the second weekend in a row. We have been a part of our church community since the very FIRST day we entered Georgia nearly thirty-three years ago.

April 28, 2014

~ Another new day...in life each new day can come with new challenges...never truer for us than the past week has been. But with that comes the knowledge that God is with us throughout each day and we must pray always to remain faithful to Him. To hold HIS hand and realize that HE is already there in the future...we have to stay in the moment. Thanking God today for two of Loren's friends who will be beside him, sharing time and fellowship with him while I have to be away from him. We are not going to have to do this alone. Love to you all.

~ "Cherish"...it's a funny word. Do you ever wonder what that word really means? The definition of the word is: "To protect and care for lovingly. To adore, hold dear, love, be devoted to"... You get the picture. I have never been clearer on what it means then at this present time. Having spent the entire past week in the hospital beside Loren, protecting and loving him and helping him to the best of my ability through the ravages of chemo and sitting quietly next to him as he sleeps, I've had many hours to reflect on that word. And I had to be honest with myself. Have I always "cherished" Loren the way that he deserves to be "cherished"? The answer was "no". Have I always loved Loren the way that he truly deserves to be loved? The answer was "no". I am saddened by this truth, but I also know that when you have spent the past thirty-three years with the same person those things are bound to ebb and flow. So today I am praying and being thankful for the man that God gave me. Yes, HIS hand was the one who put us into each other's lives, and I am praying that HE will give me the chance to truly CHERISH Loren, to LOVE him the way he deserves to be. So while you are praying for Loren's healing today, and I know that you are because we can feel it, I ask you to send a prayer up to our Heavenly Father for your own loved ones. Your spouses, your children, your grandchildren, your significant others, that you ALWAYS remember to cherish them and love them the way they deserve. Most importantly TELL them that you do! LOVE, LOVE, LOVE you all!

*****

~ Chicken soup for the soul, or in this case for the body! So maybe it wasn't chicken soup...it was beef broth! But we have turned a corner tonight! Loren was able to stomach some broth AND some crackers and let me tell you, if you don't think that is a big deal than you would be sadly mistaken! But seriously, it was so good to finally see him eat something and his incredible and gifted oncologist who visited with us tonight has told him that tomorrow "is all about nutrition"...Loren's wish to go home will be granted if he proves he can get some food into himself. Of course Loren thinks it would be just as easy to be fed intravenously as to physically eat the food himself. Ummm, that would be a "NO!" Prayers tonight for something as simple as Loren being able to eat anything of substance tomorrow so that the doctor can consider allowing him to go home to the comfort of his own surroundings! Praising God through the good AND the bad moments! Much love to all our family and friends!

April 29, 2014

1 Chronicles 28:20
"Be strong and courageous, and do the work. Don't be afraid or discouraged by the size of the task, For the Lord God, my God, is with you."

~ What is that saying? "Take two steps forward and one step back?" Yes, I think that is it. Even so, that is still moving forward. Last night was a milestone for Loren, but this morning the queasiness is again settling in and I can see the discouragement in his face. This passage is as much for me as it is for him. Last night I was so hopeful that he had turned the corner and that today he would feel energized and ready to feed his body and soul. Not so much. My friends always tell me "be specific in your prayer requests." So here it is, "Heavenly Father, be with Loren in his pain, sorrow and disappointment. Give him the strength to be able to nourish his body so that his spirit can be nourished as well. We know that through YOU all things are possible and we thank YOU and praise YOU for walking with us through this time." Sending love to all of you for your continued prayers and support for us.

April 30, 2014

~ "There's no place like home." We are so happy to be home to begin our "new normal". We don't have a clue as to what that "new normal" is going to look like and other realities are beginning to set in, but we're going to do the best we can.

MAY 2014

May 3, 2014

~ Feeling Grateful, Thankful, and Blessed. With each new day since Loren's diagnosis I have realized that I never truly knew what those words meant. Today we ventured out to our church for the annual parish picnic. We are "grateful" for an absolutely glorious day to be among our church family and we are "thankful" for Loren feeling strong enough physically and emotionally to enjoy it. We are extremely "blessed" by the many hugs, warm wishes and prayers that have been extended to us. We feel especially "blessed" to be a part of a community that prays together as well as plays together, and it felt so wonderful to be with them today. Father we thank YOU and are so grateful to YOU for leading us to our church family more than 30 years ago. We thank YOU also for the gift of Father John in our lives, who has been a loving support not just in this time of difficulty for our family, but who has been a friend for more than 20 years. Continue to bless Father John in his work with our parish family. We are grateful for this spectacular day and the fellowship we had the opportunity to share...WE ARE BLESSED.

May 4, 2014

~ Grateful, Thankful and Blessed,

It continues...thirty-three years ago this weekend Loren and I drove our U-Haul trailer into the state of Georgia. We had been married for six months and Loren had just been hired by Delta Air Lines. We were just beginning our lives together. It was a Saturday afternoon and we found a hotel and checked in. Literally, the first thing we did was pick up the phone book to see if we could find a Catholic church nearby. We found St. Philip Benizi Church and attended Mass there that Saturday evening. It has been our faith "home" from that very first night. Our parish has gone through many changes in the past thirty-three years...a new church building, many pastors and an ebb and flow in the number of families who also call it "home". It is where we raised our family and where our children received their many sacraments. But the one thing that has never changed for us is the circle of love we have always felt there, and never more so than this morning. We were asked before Mass if we would like Loren to be prayed over after Mass. Of course the answer was yes. We went into the Blessed Sacrament Chapel, a place where Loren has spent many hours with our Lord and the prayers were led by a beautiful servant of God, Sue. When she was finished and we looked up the chapel was nearly full with so many of our "family" we have come to know over the past thirty-three years. The Holy Spirit is so alive within this community of faith! Praise God from whom all blessings flow! Another reminder for me today of what it is to be "Grateful, Thankful and Blessed". We are overwhelmed by the love, prayers and concern that continue to be showered upon us. We love you all!

May 5, 2014

Romans 15:13
"May the God of hope fill you with all joy and peace as you trust in HIM, so you may overflow with hope by the power of the Holy Spirit."

~ Early this morning I spent time talking with my Mom. Some of you may know this, most may not. My Dad's health has been failing for several years and in the past year it has become more serious. Decisions had to be made that were very difficult. My Mom is a rock and through these last two weeks, regardless of how difficult her own life has been, she has been a rock for me as well. I have had my moments of strength and my moments where I have let fear and anxiety creep in and take over. I have had moments of asking "why" and not understanding why a man like my husband (and those of you who know him understand where I am coming from) has to travel this journey. When I said this to my Mom this morning she told me that early on in my Dad's illness she would ask the same question. And then one day she asked herself, "Why not?" As humans sooner or later we will all experience those times in our lives where we will be asking "why". After speaking with my Mom I walked outside and soaked in the beautiful spring morning realizing that I hadn't really been able to experience this peacefulness and calmness for quite some time. Then I saw a beautiful rose. I got my camera to capture it so I would be reminded that even in times of sadness and difficulty there is beauty and hope to be found in every situation, and in every day. Today Loren had his first follow up appointment with his neuro-oncologist and neuro-surgeon since his first treatment a couple of weeks ago. PRAISING GOD FOR THESE TWO AMAZING INSTRUMENTS OF HEALING! They were so impressed with the progress Loren has made in just a short time. Dr. Dunbar called him a "SUPERSTAR"! Oh he is! Every day he improves by leaps and bounds and they are certain that the first chemo treatment has done EXACTLY what they had hoped for. We learned so much today that we didn't know last week. We learned about the type of lymphoma Loren has. It is "large diffuse B cell", and it is extremely aggressive...scary right? I thought so too. Until Dr. Dunbar explained that it responds well to treatment. Also, that the improvements that we have seen in Loren in the last week are not because of the steroids he has been taking to bring down the swelling, but because the tumor has actually already shrunk with the first treatment! They have not seen it by MRI or CT scan, but they can tell by his physical and mental improvements. Our God is an AWESOME GOD! Today as I experienced the new life in my backyard in the beauty of the lovely flower, I know that it is also possible to experience new life in our hearts and souls and through the love of God and the Holy Spirit. Asking continued prayers for Loren and our family and sending love to you all!

May 6, 2014

Isaiah 40:31
"But those who hope in the Lord will renew their strength. They will soar on wings like eagles; they will run and not grow weary. They will walk and not be faint."

~ Another beautiful day and another day to be amazed by the wonder of our God and how much things can change in a weeks' time. So many times in the past two weeks in the many conversations we have had with family and friends I have shared the seriousness of Loren's condition right before he went to the ER on Holy Saturday. I have said that I didn't believe there would have been a Monday morning had we not gone. Until yesterday while visiting his doctors I didn't realize how true that statement was. Without even making that comment one of his doctors said, "He would not be here right now." It sent a chill up my spine, but I am so thankful for our children and our daughter-in-law, the catalysts that sent us to the hospital. If you had seen Loren those last few days before this journey began you would understand the unbelievable joy it brings me to be able to share these thoughts with you! Pickin' up sticks out in the backyard today! Who would believe that it would be such a milestone?! "Soaring on wings like eagles"! "Running and not growing weary"...okay, maybe a little weary! It did Loren such good to be outside on yet another glorious day and doing what his doctor told him to do. She told him to take time to do the things that need to be done...keep busy, active and feeling as if he has purpose. Pickin' up sticks! Yup, just pickin' up sticks! A major accomplishment and praising God who has renewed his spirit and has given him strength! What a day! Love you all and continue the prayers! We can see and feel the results of them!

May 7, 2014

~ Each day that passes brings a truer understanding of just how miraculous God's healing touch is. With each day that goes by we see HIS healing touch in Loren. Although Loren has lost twenty pounds since his diagnosis three weeks ago he continues to get stronger and feeling better every day. If you had seen Loren a few weeks ago you would have seen that he could barely walk without becoming completely exhausted and now he wants to walk around our block which would be a mile! THAT would be quite amazing and frankly nothing short of a miracle given that the second day of chemo in the hospital he looked at me and said, "I don't think I can do this." Today, as we took a walk, we talked about how strange and difficult it is to say the word "cancer". This invisible adversary that was trying so hard to take over his body is now being held at bay by modern medicine and the talents of the doctors that God placed in our lives Holy Saturday. Loren continues to improve by leaps and bounds and it makes it hard to even believe that he is ill. What a testament to the many prayers being lifted up to our Father and the laying on of hands! Praise God! Please always try to remember each day that there are people who daily are fighting a battle...it may very well be invisible to you. Whether it is a physical ailment or an emotional one, we may not be aware of it. But if we choose to live the way Jesus taught us to live you may be HIS Light to that person that day. "The Spirit of God is upon me, HE has anointed me"....love this verse in this song. Asking continued prayers for Loren. We love you all!

May 8, 2014

~ As Loren sits here this evening he is opening more cards that he received in the mail today. Every time that he receives a card in the mail and reads the well wishes inside...EVERY TIME...he says the same thing, "It makes me feel so good to know that people are thinking of me and praying for me. I really feel it and it just really makes me feel good." It brings a smile to my face and it makes me realize that half of the battle that anyone faces while going through any kind of crisis, whether it be physical or emotional, just knowing that there are people out there sending their love to you helps you fight each day. We thank you family and friends for making a difference in Loren's fight. Be assured that as I lay down to sleep tonight and pray for my beloved I will send up prayers for all of you as well who make a difference in our lives. Love and prayers to you all!

May 9, 2014

John 14:27
"Peace I leave you, my peace I give unto you: not as the world giveth, give I unto you. Let not your heart be troubled, neither let it be afraid."

~ Today was a day that I suppose you could say reality set in. That's not to say that we haven't been living with the reality of Loren's cancer, we have. But this morning we were really reflecting on it because we were having a conversation about just how far Loren has come in how he is feeling now as compared to how he was a little over three weeks ago. In fact he is so "normal", whatever that word may mean, that it is hard to believe he is ill at all. THAT is what prompted our discussion. Loren was sharing how well he was feeling and then he said, "...but then I remember that I have this "thing" in my head, and I know that I have to keep having treatments and I have to keep fighting." We were both a little sad as we reflected on the past year and all of the places we had traveled to and all of the things we had experienced together. Not the least of which was our daughter's wedding in December. How is it that we can go from such beautiful moments in our lives to THIS moment? We experienced such joy and then so quickly such sadness and fear and anxiety. REALITY...I know so many of you who have experienced this REALITY. One moment it is the many joys of life and the next moment such sorrow. So today I choose to reflect on John 14:27...The Lord has given us his peace....I am choosing to not let my heart be troubled and not be afraid. I am choosing to continue with Loren to find joy in each day and find that peace of heart that HE wants us to have. Praising God for his gift of peace and for all of our family and friends who continue to lift us up in prayer! May the peace of The Lord be with you all! Love you all!

May 12, 2014

Matthew 11:28
"Come to me, all you who are weary and burdened, and I will give you rest."

~ Today I am feeling "burdened and weary". I suppose it is something that is to be expected from time to time through a journey like this. But how can I? Do I have a right to? Especially when I look at and listen to Loren who continues to be so positive and so full of faith. Not that my faith has waned. I'm just tired. Physically, emotionally, and mentally. Besides keeping up with all the insurance, doctor appointments, lab work, disability paperwork, trips to the drug store etc., etc., there are the everyday mundane things of laundry, cleaning house, grocery shopping and all the other things that need to be done. I guess you could say that I hit the wall today. Then I look at my husband and realize that I have to keep going...he has to keep going...WE have to keep going! So, that's what we will do.

On that note there is some good news today. Loren's oncologist wanted him to see an ophthalmologist to be sure that there was nothing unusual lurking behind his eyes related to the brain cancer and the doctor gave his eyes a clean bill of health. There will be checks from time to time, but for now they looked great! Praise God for more good news! Tomorrow there will be lab work in preparation to begin the next round of chemo that will begin Wednesday. Loren is actually looking forward to it because he has had such incredible results from the first round that he just knows through the laying on of hands, being anointed, and the many prayers being lifted up for him that God is working wondrous things in him and for him.

So, as we prepare for another three days (at least) in the hospital we ask for continued prayers for healing, for strength and for God to "give us rest"...mind, body and soul. Love to all of you!

May 13, 2014

1 Peter 5:6-7
"Humble yourselves, therefore, under God's mighty hand, that he may lift you up in due time. Cast all your anxiety on him because he cares for you."

1 Thessalonians 5:18
"Give thanks in all circumstances, for this is God's will for you in Christ Jesus."

*****

~ The song "Thanksgiving" by pianist George Winston has been a favorite of mine for many years. It allows me, when I listen to it, to go to a peaceful place and reflect on many things. I have listened to this piece a number of times today and I have been reflecting on the last few weeks and all that has transpired. Tomorrow we will be going back to the place where in the beginning it was filled with fear and anxiety and many tears. But tomorrow will be different. Tomorrow we will be filled with hope and once again, like so many times in the last few weeks, be filled with thanksgiving for the incredible people that we will be with. Many compassionate nurses, and most importantly, the most unbelievable doctor who just by her very presence brings us peace of mind, heart and soul. We are so BLESSED! In THANKSGIVING to our loving Father who has placed us in their care! We ask for continued prayers for Loren as he begins his next treatment. Love you all!

May 14, 2014

Luke 1:37
"For with God nothing shall be impossible."

~ Each day that we have walked this journey since April 19th has been an experience of many emotions and learning so much about ourselves as individuals and as a couple. Even after nearly thirty-four years of marriage there has been so much to learn about one another. I can't speak for what Loren has learned about me, but what I have learned about my husband is his unbelievable strength of mind, body and faith. I always knew those attributes were there and that they were strong, but I never really knew how strong. Our faith has increased immensely, mine especially, and today is yet one more reminder about how "with God all things are possible". Our first experience in the hospital from diagnosis through the first chemo treatment was horrendous and the only thing that carried us through was the constant feeling of being lifted in prayer by our family and friends. In the past couple of weeks while home strengthening Loren's body and mind our prayer has been for his next treatment to be a much better experience than the first. Today is day one of three days of treatment and he has done BEAUTIFULLY! PRAISE GOD! He has had hardly any queasiness and has been able to eat everything put in front of him! HUGE difference from someone who couldn't even look at broth the last time he was here! Our God continues to work wondrous deeds for Loren and we will continue to believe that ALL things ARE POSSIBLE through HIM! Love to you all and please continue to lift Loren up in prayer!

May 15, 2014

Psalm 66:8
"You, Oh God, make the dawn and the sunset shout for joy."

~ Day two of Loren's second round of chemo...How many times can we say, "The Lord has done wondrous things"? An infinite number of times, that's how many! If we could we would climb to the top of the hospital and "shout for joy"! What another amazing day! Loren can't stop doing laps around the hallways! He continues to say how good he is feeling and he looks even better! He has lost his appetite a bit this evening, but he made himself eat most of his dinner because he knows how important it is to keep his strength up. The physical therapist came in today and Loren was sitting on his bed with his sweat pants on and his tennis shoes on his feet. When she walked in and introduced herself to him as his PT he jumped up off the bed and said "Oh! I've been waiting for you!" Her reaction? "What am I doing here?" They went out in the hallway where Loren did some more laps and she gave him a glowing report! Tomorrow is step three in round two and it may be a little tougher...but this man is up for the challenge! What an inspiration he is to me as well as all of his nurses and his doctor! Along with me and all of you, he prays without ceasing and our God is ever near, keeping him strong body, mind and spirit, and most especially his faith. Praising God for the beauty of this day and bringing us to the glory of the sunset "shouting with joy"! Love to all of you and thank you for your continued prayers!!!

May 17, 2014

~ We don't know the end of this journey, but we are choosing to trust in The Lord as we walk through it. We do not know what is going to come our way, but we feel comfort in knowing that our Lord is with us and we can feel all of you as you walk with us. We are home after four days in the hospital for Loren's second chemo treatment...two down. This treatment was so much better than the first, but by mid-day on day three Loren was beginning to feel the effects. He was not horribly nauseated but he did comment from time to time that his stomach just "didn't feel right", and also he began to comment that he was starting to feel tired. I had to keep reminding him that he was going through chemo and that he was going to feel tired, foggy and "just not right", and that he shouldn't be so hard on himself. Through it all he read scripture and many prayers written for people going through illnesses and cancer and praying the rosary. His faith grows ever stronger and it continues to carry him through day by day. He amazes me with his strength. We are happy to be home and looking forward to a good night sleep in our own bed and praying he will feel refreshed and stronger in the morning. Asking that you continue to keep Loren in prayer each day!

May 20, 2014

Philippians 4:13
"I can do everything through HIM who gives me strength."

~ Yet one more beautiful day on this journey! While Loren hasn't seemed to have the energy, and I use that term lightly, that he had last week, he continues to walk each day full of faith in The One who gives him strength of mind, body and spirit. This morning while I spent time in the kitchen preparing a number of meals to help make life easier for us I suggested he go out and take a little walk because it was so pretty outside. So off he went...only to show up later announcing that he had done it! He had walked a complete mile around the block without stopping! Now I am certain some of you may be thinking, "Okay, it's a mile." Well, considering a month before he ended up in the ER he could barely walk and he has had long chemo treatments twice in a two week period of time, it's a pretty big deal! He remains prayerful asking our Father in heaven to strengthen and heal his body and in turn our Father gives him the strength to do the things he must do to enable him to stay strong through this fight. I continue to be amazed by his faith and by his ability to walk through each new day with hope and grace. We are so thankful for yet another day of learning, loving and living! Pray without ceasing!

May 23, 2014

"Have patience with all things, but, first of all with yourself." ~ Saint Francis de Sales

~ So today was not a good day...for me, not so much Loren. I knew it was bound to happen. It hasn't really happened since the first week of Loren's diagnosis...that would be a meltdown. If you have ever had or known someone who has been diagnosed with a serious illness you know how your entire life revolves around it. Nearly every thought, every decision that you make, and nearly all of your activities have to do with the fact that someone in your life is dealing with a serious illness. Our days since April 19th have been filled with phone calls to doctors' offices, trips to the drug store, phone calls with disability and insurance companies and on and on. Days in the hospital for chemo treatments turn into hospital visits for lab work post and pre chemo visits. Then there is just the everyday mundane stuff like, grocery shopping, laundry, cleaning the house, etc. etc. I'm not really complaining, it just has become our reality. The truth is I wouldn't have it any other way, because as Loren's surgeon said, he wouldn't be here if things had not transpired the way that they had. But today, and I'm angry at myself for letting it happen, I lost complete patience with a situation. We had to go have pre chemo blood work done. Afterward we went and just hung out at Target (enjoyable) before grocery shopping. While there Loren got a phone call from the oncologist's office. The bloodwork hadn't been drawn correctly at the lab and we were going to have to go back and have it redrawn. I kind of blew a gasket. When your life becomes all about doctor visits, hospital visits and lab visits the last thing you want to do is have to go back and do it all over again! So tonight I imagine I am going to be asking for extra forgiveness for my lack of patience and the fact that this isn't about me....it's about my husband, who as usual, showed his "patience of a saint" side... because he is a saint and everyone knows it! He now, as he always has been all these years, is the calming force that God knew all those years ago was needed and continues to be needed in my life. We're going to do this...with God's help and continued prayers; we are going to do this! Love to you all!

May 25, 2014

Psalm 34: 4
"I sought the Lord and He answered me and delivered me from all my fears."

*****

Jesus Calling ~
"The world is too much with you, My child. Your mind leaps from problem to problem to problem, tangling your thoughts in anxious knots. When you think like that, you leave Me out of your world-view and your mind becomes darkened. Though I yearn to help, I will not violate your freedom. I stand silently in the background of your mind, waiting for you to remember that I am with you. When

you turn from your problems to My Presence, your load is immediately lighter. Circumstances may not have changed, but we carry your burdens together. Your compulsion to "fix" everything gives way to deep, satisfying connection with Me. Together we can handle whatever this day brings."

~ "Jesus Calling" is speaking directly to me and how my heart feels today. Actually, how my heart feels many days. Each day since Loren's diagnosis and since he came home from his first hospitalization and started feeling better we wake up and lay in bed talking about "stuff". It varies from day to day, but the one thing that has not varied at all for me is that within minutes of us laying there talking the reality of what is happening in our lives right now lowers itself on my heart and on my mind. If I let "it", and "it" tries VERY hard to do so, I could allow "it" to take over every part of me. The fear of the "what if's" could absolutely paralyze my every thought and every part of my being. Then I close my eyes and I remember to pray and ask our God to be with Loren and with me. To let me feel HIS presence in my heart and in my mind so that I can be present for Loren. I listen to Loren and his plans for the future and hear the strength that God is giving him because of his faith in what HE has done and in what HE WILL do! So BE GONE SATAN! You will NOT win! You will NOT make me doubt that our God is with us ALWAYS in this journey! HE is walking beside us every step of the way! As in the gospel reading today...

John 14:18
"I will not leave you as orphans, I will come to you!"

~ We will not walk this journey in fear because we know HE walks with us!

May 27, 2014

Psalm 138: 1-3, 7-8
"I give thee thanks, O LORD, with my whole heart; before the gods I sing thy praise; I bow down toward thy holy temple and give thanks to thy name for thy steadfast love and thy faithfulness; for thou hast exalted above everything thy name and thy word. On the day I called, thou didst answer me, my strength of soul thou didst increase. Though I walk in the midst of trouble, thou dost preserve my life; thou dost stretch out thy hand against the wrath of my enemies, and thy right hand delivers me. The LORD will fulfill his purpose for me; thy steadfast love, O LORD, endures forever. Do not forsake the work of thy hands."

~ As Loren is being prepared for his third round of chemo he remains steadfast in prayer. His reading for this morning is so meaningful and as usual speaking directly to how he is feeling at this time. God most definitely is stretching out HIS hand against Loren's "enemy". This "adversary" as Dr. Dunbar likes to refer to Loren's cancer is up against THE MOST POWERFUL FORCE there is! There is no doubt that The Lord has a purpose for each of us and most definitely for Loren! Though he "walks in the midst of trouble" he remains a good and faithful servant of God. Please continue to lift up prayers for Loren's continued strength and strong health as he continues this journey!

May 29, 2014

Jesus Calling ~
"I am with you, watching over you constantly. I am
Emmanuel (God with you); My Presence enfolds you in
radiant Love. Nothing, including the brightest blessings
and the darkest trials, can separate you from Me. Some of
My children find Me more readily during dark times,
when difficulties force them to depend on Me. Others feel
closer to Me when their lives are filled with good things.
They respond with thanksgiving and praise, thus opening
wide the door to My Presence.
I know precisely what you need to draw nearer to Me. Go
through each day looking for what I have prepared for
you. Accept every event as My hand-tailored provision for
your needs. When you view your life this way, the most
reasonable response is to be thankful. Do not reject any of
My gifts; find Me in every situation."

~ Oh how "Jesus Calling" has had so many messages for me! I have been coming home each evening this round of Loren's chemo because our daughter and son-in-law are here visiting...and because Loren, as always, is thinking of me and doesn't want me staying at the hospital sleeping on those horrible pull out chairs. I guess he doesn't realize that that is where I really want to be while he goes through this journey. While driving home last night I was sharing with Marie and Michael a post I had read on Facebook about someone that I know retiring and how they are moving to the "next chapter of their lives". I commented to them that I wish I could say that, and that I didn't feel like I had even begun to write the first chapter of my life, never mind having the opportunity to "move on to the next chapter". That I was still waiting. Those of you who know me and know the journey I have traveled, especially the last few years, being bumped from place to place in my job and feeling like I am just trying to find that place where I "belong" has been challenging. I try to keep reminding myself that God places you where he needs you most, that we all not only have lessons to learn, but we have lessons we need to teach as well. I haven't quite figured that out yet, but I know it's "all in God's timing".

After making that comment my son-in-law said, "Well I would say raising four children was a pretty good chapter to write." Why is it that our children at times are so much wiser than we are? To that my daughter said, "And now you are walking this journey along with Dad which is your next chapter". Maybe so, but I sure would love to be able to do some MAJOR editing to this chapter!

So, after reading today's "Jesus Calling" lines to add to my current chapter will be, "HE knows EXACTLY what I need to drawer closer to HIM and that HE already has things prepared for me"! I have to learn to "be still and listen" and know that HE is already there in my future. I have to learn patience! Never one of my strong suits, but I'm trying very hard every day.

Loren's chemo round is going well; his tests results are coming back excellent according to Dr. Dunbar's visit last night. Best of all, Dr. Dunbar is scheduling an MRI before he leaves the hospital. Pray as we have been praying, that as in Dr. Dunbar's words, "WE have been doing the PISSING OFF" to this insidious disease! Love you all and hoping that whatever chapter YOU are writing in your life right now you are feeling blessed as you walk YOUR journeys!

May 30, 2014

Hebrews 6:19
"We have this hope as an anchor for the soul, firm and secure."

~ Waiting....and prayerful....Loren has had the MRI...We have HOPE in The Lord that we will hear positive news today!

Exodus 15:26
"I am the Lord who heals you."

~ Lifting our hearts in prayer and THANKSGIVING! Dr. Dunbar has just come in and showed us Loren's scan from this morning! Every praise that could ever be raised to our God would be appropriate right now! Our God is an AWESOME God; HE has done GREAT THINGS for us! An AMAZING amount of cancer is GONE and Dr. Dunbar says, "His scan is showing a BETTER THAN AVERAGE improvement!" Can the praise and thanks you give to The Lord EVER be enough when you receive this kind of news?! OUR unceasing prayers go on and asking ALL of YOU to continue to pray for Loren and his medical team who through God's hands have worked amazing works of healing!
PRAISE GOD FROM WHOM ALL BLESSINGS FLOW!

JUNE 2014

June 1, 2014

~ Loren is home from the hospital and our little grand-daughter is here spending time with us. Some wonderful medicine for Papa for sure. Loren is tired but enjoying spending time with the baby. There has been a lot of picture taking, playing outside and trips to the park.

June 4, 2014

Isaiah 26:3
"You will guard him and keep him in perfect peace whose mind is stayed on you. Because he commits himself to you, leans on you, and hopes confidently in you."

~ As I have been for all of these years, but most especially in these last few months, I am in awe of the deep faith my husband has and continues to have in our Lord. Absolutely in awe…

*****

Jesus Calling ~
"Welcome challenging times as opportunities to trust Me. You have Me beside you and My Spirit within you, so no set of circumstances is too much for you to handle. When the path before you is dotted with difficulties, beware of measuring your strength against those challenges. That calculation is certain to riddle you with anxiety. Without Me, you wouldn't make it past the first hurdle! The way to walk through demanding days is to grip My hand tightly

and stay in close communication with Me. Let your
thoughts and spoken words be richly flavored with trust
and thankfulness. Regardless of the day's problems, I can
keep you in perfect Peace as you stay close to Me."

~ The last few days have been interesting...for lack of a better word. We have had our little granddaughter staying with us. She came the day after Loren's last chemo treatment ended, so we have been in full "Lala and Papa" mode for the last several days. While Loren was still in the hospital for his chemo I noticed a change in his energy level and in his spirit and those changes have continued into this week. Usually after a day or so of being home there is improvement in those things so it has been of some concern to me. Of course there is the fact that we have been chasing around our 18 month old granddaughter and I'M exhausted so I know that he must be feeling that as well, but I can't help but feel there is something "lurking" just under the surface.

So when I opened "Jesus Calling" this morning you might imagine how these words spoke to me. It would be so easy to let my anxieties and fears grab hold of me when I look at Loren and see the fatigue in his face and in the way his body has been moving the last couple of days. Praying for that "perfect peace" that can only be found in my trust that our Lord has and continues to hold Loren in the palm of HIS hand, and that I can continue to hold that knowledge in my heart. Please continue to pray for Loren's health and for us to continue to find the strength to walk on this journey...physically, emotionally and spiritually. And please remember that while life goes on "normally" for so many, there are so many others whose lives are being made more difficult by the death of a loved one or loss of their health in one way or another. Remember that they feel isolated and need you to remember them. Send a note, make a phone call to them and let them know they are in your heart and minds and prayers. It means the world to them...trust me.

June 5, 2014

~ I am trying so very hard to choose JOY each day...

June 9, 2014

"I plead with you, never ever give up on hope, never doubt, never tire, and never become discouraged. Be not afraid." St. John Paul II

~ As Catholics we believe in the Communion of Saints and we call upon them often to intercede for us in prayer to our Father in Heaven. It is one of "those things" often misunderstood and questioned by those of other faiths. Often it is frowned upon, but when I am asked about it my response is always, "How does that differ from asking our friends and family to keep us in prayer?"... It doesn't. But these individuals are recognized by the Catholic Church not only for the lives they lived here while on earth, but the proven miracles attributed to them after their deaths.

For weeks prior to Loren's diagnosis of brain cancer I felt in my heart and gut that there was something very serious happening. Every night when I would go to bed and begin praying I felt myself calling upon St. John Paul, who at that time had not been canonized, but I knew that there had been miracles of healing attributed to his intercession. I would ask him to intercede to our Father in Heaven and bring healing to Loren and peace of mind and heart to us both. Since Loren's diagnosis those prayers have continued along with the prayers of our family and friends and we just KNOW that is why we received the news we received less than two weeks ago after having completed only two chemo treatments.

This past week has been exhausting. Loren is beginning to feel the effects of the chemo more than he previously has, but we continue to pray with all of you, the Communion of Saints and most importantly our Father in Heaven that Loren's miraculous healing continues....YES, I used that word MIRACULOUS and that he does not suffer anything more negative with his treatment other than fatigue! We love you all!

June 10, 2014

Psalm 62:5
"Find rest, O my soul, in God alone; my hope comes from Him."

~ "BE STRONG"... these words can pertain to so many things. These words can be used to speak about the body, the mind, ones spirit or ones faith. Sometimes, as is the case with someone going through a serious illness, it can pertain to ALL of the above. Not just for the patient but for their significant other and for their family. It seems to be the case for Loren right now. I noticed a difference in him last week. There is a fatigue of mind and body, noticeably in his face and the movement of his body. Yesterday, even before beginning his chemo treatment, he was not feeling well. I'm not quite sure if it is a mind over matter thing or that we really didn't have much down time in between chemo treatments this time around. His faith never seems to waiver. He remains prayerful day after day. We both do. However, this morning as I made yet another phone call for yet another doctor appointment he commented, "I probably won't be going back to work this year." This year? The spirit is weakening. He has gone from "I want to get back to work" nearly EVERY day since his first chemo treatment to not even really mentioning it in this past week...until this morning....in a negative way. Even though his oncologist shared that all of his blood work was stellar AND was giving us "hypotheticals" yesterday on having only 4-6 more treatments...again, only hypothetically. Who knows...but for God. And how beautiful and how MIRACULOUS that would be as when we started this journey back in April we were looking at possibly a YEAR of treatments! GOD IS GOOD!

Please continue to pray for strength of mind and body for Loren....and for me. And continue to let Loren know by messages and calls that he is not alone. That he is not forgotten and that he continues to be prayed for. He needs that...WE need that. Love to you all!

June 11, 2014

Psalm 28: 7
"The Lord is my strength and my shield; my heart trusts
in Him, and I am helped. Therefore my heart rejoices, and
I praise Him with my song."

~ It's the dawn of a new day and todays devotion in Jesus Calling is speaking loud and clear to me once again! And our God has shown to us yet one more time who is in control. Lift your eyes and your voices and ask HIM to be with you, to strengthen you, to fill you with peace and it is given to you. By the end of yesterday Loren was feeling renewed in spirit and although he hasn't really been eating as well as he has previously he would tell me that "I am feeling so much better!" PRAISING GOD WHO IS ALWAYS THERE FOR US! We only have to remember that and call upon HIM! Like the words from Jesus Calling reminded us..."the battle for control of your mind is fierce"...it would be so easy to give in to that, to lose hope when you are not feeling strong of mind and body, but we WILL NOT! We remember daily who is in control and we know that the answer is prayer. YOURS and OURS! Love to you all and continue to lift Loren in prayer!

June 16, 2014

Proverbs 3:5
"Trust in the Lord with all your heart and lean not on your own understanding."

~ "Trust in The Lord"...so many times in the last couple of months, I am not afraid to admit, my trust has wavered. Sad, but true. I am a human being and there have been days where I most definitely was aware of the darkness and evil that wants to take over the trust that I, that WE have had all our lives and through this journey in our Lord. Loren's illness and my own personal trials could have easily taken their toll. But in the last couple of weeks with the incredible news that we received from Dr. Dunbar we were reminded once again that the darkness WILL NOT overtake us. Today, I am full of gratitude for answered prayers once again in my own personal journey. Thank you Father for ALWAYS being there in my future... I will ALWAYS walk through my days knowing YOU are out there WAY AHEAD OF ME!

June 17, 2014

~ Today after many months of illness my father received the ultimate "peace of mind". He went "HOME" this evening. My heart is breaking...for so many reasons.

My sister was there to witness this moment after my Dad's passing. All of his life he would say when we would ask what he would like for any special occasion, his birthday, Father's Day, Christmas whatever the occasion was, he would always say, "Peace of Mind."

This framed statement hung in his room at the nursing home. My Mom made his room as beautiful and comfortable as possible...as close to being "home" as could be. Forty-five minutes after his passing and after a horrendous storm a beacon of light came through the window and illuminated this piece that hung next to his bed.

Look closely... There is also a cross. He is "HOME"...and he has received the ultimate "Peace of Mind"! "God Bless you good and faithful servant". You are HOME!

"Peace of Mind"

June 18, 2014

Jesus Calling ~
"You are My beloved child. I chose you before the
foundation of the world, to walk with Me along paths
designed uniquely for you. Concentrate on keeping in step
with Me, instead of trying to anticipate My plans for you.
If you trust that My plans are to prosper you and not to
harm you, you can relax and enjoy the present moment.
Your hope and your future are rooted in heaven, where
eternal ecstasy awaits you. Nothing can rob you of your
inheritance of unimaginable riches and well-being.
Sometimes I grant you glimpses of your glorious future, to
encourage you and spur you on. But your main focus
should be staying close to Me. I set the pace in keeping
with your needs and My purpose."

~ When I read these words this morning my Dad was front and center in my thoughts and prayers. His hope was for sure "rooted in heaven, where eternal ecstasy awaits you." He was a faithful man, and I am proud to say I married a man just like my father, strong in faith, no matter the circumstances. For sure today, he is experiencing THE "eternal ecstasy" and one of my friends reminded me this morning, "whole again" and has received that "Peace of Mind" he longed for all of his life. I feel he always knew that he would truly only receive that gift at the end of his life when he would leave his physical body and was welcomed "HOME". I love you Dad.

June 19, 2014

"He will raise you up on eagle's wings, bear you on the breath of dawn, make you to shine like the sun, and hold you in the palm of His hand."- Michael Joncas

~ This song has always been a favorite of mine. As I lay in bed last night after praying this song played in my head, and as I woke in and out of sleep it was almost as if it was on continuous play. So strange how God works to comfort you in times of trouble or grief. I'm not clear if it is a message from God that HE has my Dad with HIM, or it is a message from my Dad letting me know without a doubt that he is with God. Possibly it is just God's way of blessing us with that knowledge. Since the beginning of April life in my world has been challenging both emotionally and spiritually. A journey in every sense of the word. Along the way I have been lifted in prayer... WE have been lifted in prayer, and I keep sharing with everyone that until you are on the receiving end of that you have no idea just how powerful that truly is. My father was a quiet man, one of very few words. He was a prayerful man who loved his Catholic faith with all his heart. He didn't have to SAY it, he lived it. It showed in the type of man he was. He was true to his faith and to God, faithful to his family and in the workplace. He had a love and devotion to his wife that only few women could dream of. I know this because I witnessed that love and because of it I married a man with the same love of his faith and a love and devotion to his wife and family that my father had. I pray that if my Dad didn't know that is how I felt about him in life, he knows it now in death. I am thankful for my sister who was by my Dad's side so that I was able to tell him one last time that I loved him because I couldn't be there at his side as he went HOME. I believe that this song has played in my head as a message to let me know that my Dad is indeed "in the palm of HIS hand" at this time. He has his "Peace of Mind". I ask your continued prayers for Loren and for myself and for my family. I also ask you to pray for my Mom who has been a rock throughout her journey and has been an example to me in mine these last couple of months.

June 20, 2014

Jesus Calling ~
"I speak to you continually. My nature is to communicate, though not always in words. I fling glorious sunsets across the sky, day after day after day. I speak in the faces and voices of loved ones. I caress you with a gentle breeze that refreshes and delights you. I speak softly in the depths of your spirit, where I have taken up residence. You can find Me in each moment, when you have eyes that see and ears that hear. Ask My Spirit to sharpen your spiritual eyesight and hearing. I rejoice each time you discover My Presence. Practice looking and listening for Me during quiet intervals. Gradually you will find Me in more and more of your moments. You will seek Me and find Me, when you seek Me above all else."

~ My father has attained the "Peace of Mind" he had longed for all of his life, knowing full well that it would never be attained until he had gone "HOME" to his Father in heaven. The above quote taken from today's Jesus

Calling is so very appropriate. There are "no coincidences" in the moments of communications from my father. They are moments of "glorious sunsets across the sky" and "a gentle breeze that caresses" ~ all ways for us to be aware that in death there is new life and my father is surely experiencing his new life. We were blessed this evening to have been together as a family as person after person came to honor my father at his calling hours. His legacy was far reaching not just within his family. Although in today's world the words "honesty" and "integrity" are two words that are rarely used, we heard them in abundance tonight, and I am proud to say that they were used to describe our father over and over again. It has been a long time since I referred to myself as "Daddy's little girl", but in my heart, I have always thought that, and I am proud to say he was my "Daddy". I pray he knows it. Tomorrow...actually today, as it is the dawn of a new day, we will lay our father to rest. It has been a long journey for him, one that no one should ever have to endure, but he IS at peace, this I know.

June 21, 2014

Numbers 6: 24-26
"The Lord bless you and keep you; the Lord make his face shine upon you and be gracious to you; the Lord turn his face toward you and give you peace."

~ It was a beautiful celebration of my father's life today. We are blessed.

June 24, 2014

Hebrews 11: 1
"Now faith is the substance of things hoped for, the
evidence of things not seen.
Psalm 61: 2
"When my heart is overwhelmed lead me to the rock that
is higher than I."

~ I am back home in Georgia and it is time to give everything to my husband...

June 26, 2014

~ Loren has been taken for his MRI. We thank you for your prayers that have been a constant and have lifted us up. Please offer up a prayer that we will continue to see God's hand at work in his healing....miracles ARE possible! Love to you all!

*****

Jesus Calling ~
"Stay calmly conscious of Me today, no matter what.
Remember that I go before you as well as with you into
the day. Nothing takes Me by surprise. I will not allow
circumstances to overwhelm you, so long as you look to
Me. I will help you cope with whatever the moment
presents. Collaborating with Me brings blessings that far
outweigh all your troubles. Awareness of My Presence
contains Joy that can endure all eventualities."

~ I was struck by these words this morning and now they make perfect sense. "Stay calmly conscious of ME today, no matter what." When I read these words this morning I thought to myself, "I'm not sure what is going to happen today, but yes, HE is already there." Loren's MRI results came in. The word is "stable". No changes...no better, but no worse. PRAISE GOD. At first I cried, I was so disappointed. There was such incredible news with the first MRI. But then I realized that today's Jesus Calling was letting me know once again that God is already there. HE already knew what would be seen. Although it was not what I wanted to hear I realize that Loren is BLESSED in that he is doing well and tolerating his treatments. And so I ask once again, please continue to keep Loren and me in prayer, to sustain our strength mind, body and spirit. Love to you all.

*****

~ It has been ten days since my father died and today he is on my mind a lot. Many times in the past week it was said that my Dad was a man of very few words. So when he said something you knew it was from the heart and of great substance. Like on October 11, 1980, the day Loren and I married. He spoke words I will never forget. As he got ready to walk me down the aisle he looked down at me and said, "I could not have done better for you if I had hand-picked Loren for you myself." It still brings tears to my eyes when I think of it. One important man in my life is gone; the other is fighting an unbelievable battle for his life. Father in Heaven give me strength.

JULY 2014

July 1, 2014

~ For the past couple of weeks I have struggled with "the storms of adversity" and although I have been prayerful I have found it easier to give into fear and anxiety and sadness. Ever thankful for the right words to come my way when they are needed most, my sister and her husband hold in their hearts their favorite saying "GOD IS GOOD" and shared them with me today. I must hold them in mine as well.

Dr. Dunbar called yesterday afternoon and we had a long conversation with her. As is her way, she was reassuring in tone and in her information to us and we were reminded that Loren's journey...our journey, is not going to be over next week. We need to be thankful for the progress he has made AND that he has remained healthy during his treatment. Praising God this morning for that, and for HIS prompting Dr. Dunbar to call and share her reassurance and wisdom with us.

Continue to keep Loren in prayer that he remains healthy and that we stay strong mind, body and spirit. Love to you all.

July 10, 2014

Jesus Calling ~
"Relax in My peaceful Presence. Do not bring
performance pressures into our sacred space of
communion. When you are with someone you trust
completely, you feel free to be yourself. This is one of the

joys of true friendship. Though I am Lord of lords and King of kings, I also desire to be your intimate Friend. When you are tense or pretentious in our relationship, I feel hurt. I know the worst about you, but I also see the best in you. I long for you to trust Me enough to be fully yourself with Me. When you are real with Me, I am able to bring out the best in you: the very gifts I have planted in your soul. Relax, and enjoy our friendship."

~ If, like me, you sometimes wonder "What is my connection, my relationship with God and HIS Son all about? Do THEY hear me when I cry out to THEM? How do THEY feel when my faith and trust in THEM wanes?" Then I open up Jesus Calling... Oh THEY KNOW and THEY KNOW ME and ACCEPT me with all my faults and transgressions. It has been a tough few days, a tough couple of weeks. Who am I kidding? It's been a tough few months! Last night as I laid here in the hospital and began praying I found myself apologizing to our Father and HIS Son for my distrust, for my wavering in my faith. I asked for forgiveness and once again for them to give me strength, patience and peace and ALWAYS, ALWAYS to bring healing to Loren's body, mind and spirit. Today's Jesus Calling was a direct answer from the Father and the Son! This morning I am thankful for THEIR unending love and understanding of my failings.

July 11, 2014

~ While in the hospital we received word from our daughter and son-in-law that they were going to be deployed very shortly. We spoke with Dr. Dunbar and she worked diligently to get Loren out of the hospital as quickly as possible and she assured us that Loren would be fine to travel so that we will be able to visit with them before their deployment.

True to her word she was able to get Loren discharged from the hospital. We traveled to visit with them...it ended up being a very short trip.

July 12, 2014

~ So blessed to have been able to spend time with Marie and Michael. Sadly, Loren wasn't feeling very well and we decided to come home earlier than planned, but we are so happy to have had the opportunity to hug our girl and our son-in-law. It was pushing it for Loren to make the trip because it takes him a few days to recover from chemo but he was determined to see his girl! Asking continued prayers for Loren and most especially at this time for Marie and Michael.

July 14, 2014

Jesus Calling ~
"Keep walking with Me along the path I have chosen for you. Your desire to live close to Me is a delight to My heart. I could instantly grant you the spiritual riches you desire, but that is not My way for you. Together we will forge a pathway up the high mountain. The journey is arduous at times, and you are weak. Someday you will dance light-footed on the high peaks; but for now, your walk is often plodding and heavy. All I require of you is to take the next step, clinging to My hand for strength and

direction. Though the path is difficult and the scenery dull
at the moment, there are sparkling surprises just around
the bend. Stay on the path I have selected for you. It is
truly the path of Life."

~ The journey is most definitely arduous and I do find myself very weak and weary. I will "cling to your hand for strength and direction". Praising you today Jesus for bringing us this far...help us to trust the path we must journey.

July 15, 2014

Matthew 6:34
"Therefore do not worry about tomorrow, for tomorrow
will worry about itself. Each day has enough trouble of
its own."

~ Since the beginning of this journey there have been many different stages of emotions. The fear, the anxiety, the sadness, the loneliness and the "with God by our side, we've got this"... I could go on and on but I'm sure you get the picture. From the beginning Loren had said "I want to go back to work" daily, several times a day most of the time. Lately I have noticed that he has not been saying that very often. Last night while we ate dinner he talked with me about his concerns. He felt he needed to go back to work because we are closing in on his moving from his full pay to short term disability. Mentally I know that is what he wants, but physically I know how challenging it will be. I tried to the best of my ability to once again be "the cheerleader". "It's okay, we will be fine...I will be going back to work...we will be provided for..." Do I believe it? Yes, but as always there are those fears and anxieties that creep in. My prayer last night as I laid in bed was for God to provide for us and for Loren's peace of mind. His mind should be filled only with what he needs for healing and peace. While I sat here at the table this morning doing the bills he called up to me from downstairs. "Libby have you read "Jesus Calling" this morning?" I had not. He said "It is REALLY speaking to me this morning!" Oh yes, like SO MANY MORNINGS! Jesus once again holding out HIS hand for us to grab hold of...to give us strength, to give us courage and to show us that once again HE'S GOT THIS! We only have to keep believing.

July 24, 2014

Jesus Calling ~
"Thankfulness opens the door to My Presence. Though I am always with you, I have gone to great measures to preserve your freedom of choice. I have placed a door between you and Me, and I have empowered you to open or close that door. There are many ways to open it, but a grateful attitude is one of the most effective. Thankfulness is built on a substructure of trust. When thankful words stick in your throat, you need to check up on your foundation of trust. When thankfulness flows freely from your heart and lips, let your gratitude draw you closer to Me. I want you to learn the art of giving thanks in all circumstances. See how many times you can thank Me daily; this will awaken your awareness to a multitude of blessings. It will also cushion the impact of

trials when they come against you. Practice My Presence
by practicing the discipline of thankfulness."

~ Dear family and friends, they have come to take Loren for his MRI. Would you take a moment and say a prayer for him that God's Almighty Healing Hand has been working miracles in Loren? Thank you so much.

As I read Jesus Calling this morning while Loren was down having his MRI I couldn't help but think to myself "I need to be THANKFUL to GOD today regardless of what we hear." How did I, once again, know that Jesus Calling was speaking directly to me?

~ So here is what we know. Dr. Dunbar came in and showed us Loren's MRI scan. The news is quite spectacular, and yet disappointing at the same time, if that can be. Loren's cancer is now more than ninety percent gone! PRAISE GOD! However, there continues to be an area that is being very difficult. In fact, there seems to have been a slight bit of growth. "Rogue cells", Dr. Dunbar calls them. They don't seem to want to respond to the chemotherapy which has obliterated more than ninety percent of the cancer. So, we will be staying at the hospital today. She has ordered a stat MRI of Loren's spine, just to be certain there isn't anything lurking there. If it doesn't show anything she will do a lumbar puncture to check the spinal fluid. If those come back clean, and please PRAY, PRAY, PRAY that it does, then it will be time to change up the chemo "recipe" and possibly add gamma knife radiation to that area. We knew that this was a possibility but we were so hopeful and prayerful it would be a different story. Loren was to start having his chemo in Fayetteville his next round, but because of the new concerns we made the decision on the spot to continue his care in Atlanta under the watchful eye of Dr. Dunbar.

Dr. Dunbar has consulted with another doctor at Emory who is at the top of the field and he is in total agreement with Dr. Dunbar's assessment and on this next course of action. She also has assured us that we are still just in "Chapter One" of this story. She understands our emotions fully and she is confident in what she says is ONLY a curative scenario.

We remain so thankful to God for placing us in her care. She tells us daily that she and her team pray for Loren, for me and for our family and when we shared with her that we pray daily for her as well, her eyes teared up. THAT is a doctor who understands that all that she is, her talent, and her knowledge, comes from somewhere else, and THAT is the kind of doctor I want to be taking care of my husband, family and friends if the need should ever arise.

So we begin the next part of our journey. But as I have said, remaining ever thankful and grateful to our God who has made it clear HE is beside us with his outstretched arms holding us up, giving us strength for the road ahead. Please continue to pray.

July 25, 2014

~ Today would have been my Dad's 80th birthday...missing him.

*****

~ Loren went back downstairs for an additional MRI scan. Although we haven't spoken directly to Dr. Dunbar, she did speak with our nurse. The preliminary scans look like there is nothing to be concerned about other than a previously diagnosed herniated disc which has worsened...but hasn't really been causing any symptoms for Loren. Again, this is preliminary. So, the next step is to perform a lumbar puncture later today to rule out any cancerous cells in the spinal fluid.

We are comforted in knowing that our family and friends are with us today in thought in prayer. Thanking all of you!

*****

~ Loren has come back from his lumbar puncture. So far so good, the procedure went fine. He just has to comply with the "flat on your back or on your side" rule for the next few hours. The internal medicine doctor who was assigned to watch over Loren today for Dr. Dunbar came in and said that she and Dr. Dunbar have decided it would be best for Loren to stay in the hospital another night for observation. At this point in time (4:30PM) it only makes sense to do that. I'm not quite sure if we will receive any information tonight about the results, I would sincerely doubt it. Again, thanking you all for your love, support and prayers!

*****

...and last update for today, Dr. Dunbar just came in and showed the MRI scans from this morning. So far, these tests show no evidence of metastasis to the spine. Which is wonderful news, but of course the spinal fluid tests need to come back to be sure one hundred percent. That will probably take several days. I don't know if there are enough thanks for all of you, and to our Heavenly Father! God Bless!

July 26, 2014

~ Well, we thought we were going home this morning. Apparently Loren's lab work showed that his kidneys are not functioning at their best right now. Dr. Dunbar said they are certainly not in "the danger" zone, but she is being cautious and letting the specialists take a look at him and giving him extra fluids because she doesn't feel he could take in the volume he needs at home to flush his kidneys well. She also feels that the change in kidney function more than likely is from the dyes that were needed for all the imaging that was done yesterday. Prayers please....

*****

~ Good news, rather GREAT news is that the kidney specialist was just in to see Loren. He was spouting numbers right and left. Let's just say at this time he is not alarmed at all with the numbers he is seeing and the ultrasound of Loren's kidneys looks good. Bad news is...another night in the hospital with fluids pumping and Loren not having an appetite to eat. I'm afraid he's probably lost a good bit of weight this visit. He's barely eaten. I'm not really sure what causes it, but the moment he gets here in the hospital he doesn't want to eat. I'm going stir crazy...he does fine because he's so tired all he does is sleep. Thank God for modern technology...iPads, iPhones etc. So if anybody out there has nothing to do feel free to come up here and spend some time with me.

July 27, 2014

~ Kidneys have not recovered the way the doctors would like...another day and night in paradise...

July 28, 2014

~ Home...and he's cravin' pizza! You got it honey! As much as you can eat!

July 31, 2014

~ Now comes the time when I will try to be both caregiver and full time worker. Praying God will give me the strength to be everything Loren will need me to be.

*****

~ My heart and my soul are full of joy after being back "home on the hill"! I love my Spring Hill family and I thank them for welcoming me back with open arms!

AUGUST 2014

August 1, 2014

Isaiah 40:31
"Those who hope in the Lord will renew their strength."

~ ...and the time has come for Loren to renew his physical strength. We have put much hope in The Lord these last few months and we believe that HE has been walking this journey with us, with the nurses in the hospital and most of all Dr. Erin Dunbar. Along with our prayers, and those of our family, friends and Dr. Dunbar, Loren has come this far in his journey beautifully. As many of you know, Loren's last time in the hospital ended up being seven days rather than the usual three to four. He had developed some issues with his kidneys and Dr. Dunbar, as she always does, wanted to be sure that Loren was being taken care of for his safety and health. She called in kidney specialists and kept Loren in the hospital until she was certain it was safe for him to go home.

There are several wonderful things to share. First, Loren's cancer is more than ninety percent gone. Second, his MRI of his spine was good and third, the report we had been holding our breath for to get the results of, the biopsy of his lumbar puncture, came back with no suspicious cells. PRAISING GOD!

As we shared before, there is a spot showing in his brain MRI that Dr. Dunbar now wants to treat with radiation. She was hoping that Loren would not have to have any radiation but this spot is not responding to chemo, so she needs to take a different approach.

She is now prepared to give Loren a "chemo holiday". She will be changing the "recipe" that she is using because Loren has reached the parameters of the protocol that has been used. He reached the maximum number of treatments allowed in the chemotherapy protocol. Most people do not as they suffer adverse reactions that make it impossible to continue that particular treatment. The second parameter being that the cancer responds to treatment with more than a seventy-five percent reduction in the cancer...he's at more than ninety percent.

While Loren's body is resting, Dr. Dunbar will determine which chemo treatment to continue with and he will get the radiation. We are so thankful that God placed us in the care of Dr. Dunbar. Who would have thought that three months ago when we were told that he would be having more than a year of treatment that we would be at this point of the journey? Three months into treatment and some pretty miraculous things are happening!

There will be a number of specialists brought onto the team to work with Loren and give him the appropriate testing so that he can begin driving...AND hopefully, for his emotional well-being, be able to get back to work.

So, in the next few weeks while he is recovering the strength of his body, we ask that you continue to keep him in prayer. That God strengthen him, body, mind and spirit. That God continue to work through HIS instrument of healing, Dr. Dunbar, and that HE bring Loren to complete healing. God Bless you all!

August 4, 2014

~ A Life Lesson...or two. Since the beginning of this journey of Loren's illness several months ago Dr. Dunbar encouraged me to journal so that people we know can walk alongside us and know what we are experiencing. I have tried my best to do that. All the while feeling I was "reaching out" to those that we know.

Over the weekend I received a message from someone. I hope she will forgive me for referencing her message, but it really got me thinking about "the lesson" in this journey for me. She began by saying she was so sorry for not being there for me through the last couple of months and essentially asking me to forgive her for that. She is someone who has endured much sorrow in her own life. There is nothing to forgive. I learned a long time ago that I have to meet people where they are in their lives. And truth be known, here is one of MY lessons. I had to ask myself, "Have YOU made yourself available to those who are struggling...mentally, physically and emotionally?" I have always thought I have been there reaching out to those who need it. Perhaps not. This has been a very lonely journey. Loren and I have felt very alone, very isolated much of the time. I pray through this experience in our lives we will be more loving, more willing to give of ourselves and make ourselves more available to those that we know who are in need. That is the first life lesson I have learned. The second lesson that I have learned is that the only one I can really rely on is

God. HIS presence has been with us non-stop throughout this entire journey. HE was the one who picked me up when I was brought to my knees with Loren's diagnosis. HE was the one who sat with me in the ICU at 4AM watching Loren sleep when he was in the hospital the first long and lonely night. HE is the one who has sustained me morning, noon and night, when I was afraid to think about the "what if's". I have never lost sight of that.

I have asked HIM over and over again, "What lessons are YOU wanting me to learn Lord?" Two of them have become quite clear. To be more loving, giving and supportive when I am aware of someone else's pain, and that God is ALWAYS there holding my hand when no one else is. I am stronger because of that knowledge.

August 10, 2014

Psalm 46: 1
"God is our refuge and strength, a very present help in trouble."

Jesus Calling ~
"Relax in My healing, holy Presence. Allow Me to transform you through this time alone with Me. As your thoughts center more and more on Me, trust displaces fear and worry. Your mind is somewhat like a seesaw. As your trust in Me goes up, fear and worry automatically go down. Time spent with Me not only increases your trust; it also helps you discern what is important and what is not. Energy and time are precious, limited entities. Therefore, you need to use them wisely, focusing on what is truly

important. As you walk close to Me, saturating your mind
with Scripture, I will show you how to spend your time
and energy. My Word is a lamp to your feet; My Presence
is a Light for your path."

~ Once again The Lord who ALWAYS knows my heart had Jesus Calling open to words of wisdom, hope and strength. I have been having a difficult time finding that strength myself for several days now. After four months of us walking this journey I have become weary and at times I have given in to the weariness, the fear, the anxiety, and the sorrow of this walk. I needed to read the words in today's Jesus Calling. After several days of Loren not feeling well and experiencing a number of the same symptoms he was experiencing before his diagnosis in April he woke this morning to say, "I think we should go to the ER today." Our son who was concerned enough after my conversation with him last night had driven down from Kennesaw and arrived at our door at 10PM. He drove us up to Atlanta to the ER which was a blessing because I had barely slept all night. After a CT scan and an MRI they found that the tumor that has been resistant to treatment had grown and is causing swelling in the brain. They have begun steroid treatment again and are keeping him in the hospital. Please continue to pray for us. It has been a difficult week and we both need strength and comfort and peace through your prayers.

August 11, 2014

Ephesians 3:16-19
"I pray that out of his glorious riches he may strengthen
you with power through his Spirit in your inner being, so
that Christ may dwell in your hearts through faith. And I
pray that you, being rooted and established in love, may
have power, together with all the saints, to grasp how
wide and long and high and deep is the love of Christ, and
to know this love that surpasses knowledge—that you
may be filled to the measure of all the fullness of God."

August 12, 2014

Jesus Calling ~
"Come to Me when you are weak and weary. Rest snugly
in My everlasting arms. I do not despise your weakness,
My child. Actually, it draws Me closer to you, because
weakness stirs up My compassion—My yearning to help.
Accept yourself in your weariness, knowing that I
understand how difficult your journey has been.
Do not compare yourself with others, who seem to skip
along their life-paths with ease. Their journeys have been
different from yours, and I have gifted them with
abundant energy. I have gifted you with fragility,
providing opportunities for your spirit to blossom in My
Presence. Accept this gift as a sacred treasure: delicate,
yet glowing with brilliant Light. Rather than struggling
to disguise or deny your weakness, allow Me to bless you
richly through it."

~ Oh Heavenly Father, thank you for these words today. After only a few weeks out of treatment Loren was beginning to have a return of a number of symptoms which concerned me enough to contact Dr. Dunbar. An MRI has shown a huge recurrence of cancer. How can this be? How can this be? I am just barely back to work and now this. How do I do this? How?

August 13, 2014

Joshua 1:9
"Have I not commanded you? Be strong and courageous.
Do not be afraid; do not be discouraged for the Lord your
God will be with you wherever you go."

~ How can it be that just a few weeks ago Loren and I felt as if we had climbed to the top of the mountain and we were beginning to head over the other side and in only a few short weeks we feel as if the climb, the journey is only just beginning again? How do you hold on to something that you can't see? By believing that God is with you through every climb, every storm, every journey....by FAITH, and by knowing that WE don't know what God's will is, but that we have to accept it, no matter what HIS will may be. It is the hardest thing I have ever had to have faith in and I am struggling with it each moment of the day.

Tomorrow Loren will begin another journey. One that is certain to be a daunting one. But God has commanded us "Be strong and be brave. For the Lord God will be with you." HE has been, is, and will be with Loren and with all of us as we hold onto HIM for HIS strength. My day began as it normally does and before I left for work this morning I found myself dropped to my knees crying out to God the Father, God the Son, and God the Holy Spirit for strength for this next journey for Loren and for me, and by the time I had finished THEY had filled me with a peace that I have not felt for some time. When the emotion has overcome me throughout this day I recall that feeling and once again give thanks for the peace that can only come from believing we are not alone.

Please continue to pray and ask God to work his miracle of healing in Loren.

August 14, 2014

Psalm 46:1
"God is our refuge and strength, a very present help in trouble. Therefore we will not fear."

~ Several hours ago Loren began his new chemo treatment. A short while after I arrived at the hospital today we were met by Loren's oncologist and the doctor who runs the palliative care center here at the hospital. If you don't know what that is (I didn't) they are a department that helps families and individuals with many needs and decisions during a serious illness. It was a long and emotional visit with sobering conversation. After the doctors left Loren and I continued the conversation for a good while. What I took away from our conversation was not only because of what I could see on Loren's face but what I heard in his voice. Loren is at peace. He has given himself over to God's will, regardless of what that may be. He said it to me. He said, "As hard as it has been for me, and I still struggle with it, I have given myself over to HIS will." I have had no doubt that Loren would give himself to God in that way. His love of God and his faith was one of the things that I fell in love with when I fell in love with him all those years ago. I pray that through this journey I can be as strong in my faith and as accepting of God's will as he is. Please continue to pray that God keep him strong in body, mind and spirit through this new journey.

August 16, 2014

Isaiah 55:6
"Seek the Lord while HE may be found, call upon HIM while HE is near."

~ Seeking The Lord as we continue along this journey......a winding road along which our Lord is guiding our path.

~ Today is day three of Loren's new chemo regimen. There has been a problem with the one type of chemo being used. It keeps crystallizing and no one seems to know why. It is a bit disconcerting, but offering it up to our God to take away the additional concern it brings our way. So far Loren is tolerating it very well. At the most right now he is fatigued, but with the advances in nausea medications and other symptom medications he has done well. The steroids he has been on since last Sunday for the swelling in his brain have given him his appetite back. He has been doing a great job eating! It is important for him to keep up his strength and nutrition for this fight.

While sitting here with Loren these past couple of days he is sleeping a lot and the room is quiet, but for listening to music quietly playing I have spent a lot of time praying and reflecting on what God's plan may be...all the while realizing that I really have no clue. And while I attempt to stay focused only on God the "evil one" makes sure I am aware of his presence...always lurking. Always there attempting to weaken my heart and my soul that only wishes to be protected by God. Thoughts of the "what ifs", the "how" and the "whys" begin to swirl like a whirlpool waiting to pull me under.

Then something miraculous happens. Something unexpected...a "Godidence", like what happened last night. For some unknown reason at 11PM last night I decided it was necessary for me to pull up my email from work. Imagine what it felt like to receive an email from the principal of our school to share some wonderful news from a parent of one of the little ones in our classroom. My heart and soul were lifted with such joy! I have believed from day one when I was hired for this position that God's hand was truly in it. In this "home" there have been so many people there, loving and supporting me with prayer and open arms, and letting me know daily that "I matter"....and yet, I have struggled emotionally so much every day. Never has the struggle between God's goodness and the devil's evil been so evident to me.

So, it looks as if because of the issue with the one type of chemo and the remixing of it several times that it has delayed the starting of the final type of medication. Loren will be staying probably into the first part of the week. His spirits are good; he continues to pray without ceasing. I will look at him and he will be looking at the ceiling and I will ask him, "What are you thinking honey?", and he will answer, "I'm just praying"..."just praying"...his faith and his faithfulness growing with every minute of every day still amazes me, and I am trying my best to walk with him as it grows...as it has been all of our lives together. I have always had a hard time keeping up..."Honey, can you slow down, you're walking too fast, I can't keep up"...words I have spoken to him so many times in our almost thirty-four years of marriage...trying hard to keep up. God bless all of you. Continue to pray and walk this journey with us.

August 22, 2014

~ The last week has been a struggle in so many ways...today I was blessed by dear friends who just wanted to let me know I was being thought of. I love and appreciate all of them. We are home from the hospital.

August 23, 2014

Jesus Calling ~
"Entrust your loved ones to Me; release them into My protective care. They are much safer with Me than in your clinging hands. If you let a loved one become an idol in your heart, you endanger that one—as well as yourself. Remember the extreme measures I used with Abraham and Isaac. I took Isaac to the very point of death to free Abraham from son worship. Both Abraham and Isaac suffered terribly because of the father's undisciplined emotions. I detest idolatry, even in the form of parental love.
When you release loved ones to Me, you are free to cling to My hand. As you entrust others into My care, I am free to shower blessings on them. My Presence will go with them wherever they go, and I will give them rest. This same Presence stays with you, as you relax and place your trust in Me. Watch to see what I will do."

~ Dear God, why am I just reading this now at days end? Another reminder as to why I must try to continue to find the words to pray.

August 24, 2014

Psalm 105:4
"Look to the Lord and his strength; seek his face always."

~ Loren passed out this morning on his way to the bathroom. We are in the emergency room. They are admitting him. His bone marrow counts are bottomed out...

August 26, 2014

Psalm 105: 4
"Look to the Lord and His strength; seek His face always."

August 28, 2014

Ephesians 6:10-11
"Finally, be strong in the Lord and in the strength of HIS might. Put on the whole armor of God that you may be able to stand against the schemes of the devil."

~ Every day for more than a week I have been feeling this. I have had many conversations with a dear friend about how I feel the pull of the evil one, the darkness that it wants me to feel. I struggle at the beginning of each day to put one foot in front of the other to get out the door. Then I reach the front doors of the place that I KNOW God's hand has placed me. The place where I feel safe, comforted, loved and cared for while Loren and I fight this battle. I am so very thankful for all of these people who are surrounding me and helping me through each moment of every day.

It's going on nearly a full week of Loren being in the hospital. His bone marrow counts continue to be bottomed out, but his spirit and faith continue to soar. He amazes me, and I wish I had a fraction of the faith that I have seen in him over these past months. I want to ask that you all continue to keep Loren in prayer...praying specifically for God's healing hand to restore his blood counts...white cells, red cells and platelets and for me to continue to hold strong to God's hand and give me strength so that my spirit and faith can soar like Loren's.

August 30, 2014

"If you must look back, do so forgivingly. If you must look forward do so prayerfully. However, the wisest thing you can do is be present in the present...Gratefully."
~ Maya Angelou

~ My daughter sent this quote to me today. She is so smart, and I love her!

August 31, 2014

Proverbs 3: 5-6
"Trust in the Lord with all your heart. Do not lean on your own understanding. In all your ways acknowledge Him and He will make your paths straight."

Jesus Calling ~
"Grow strong in your weakness. Some of My children I've gifted with abundant strength and stamina. Others, like you, have received the humble gift of frailty. Your fragility

is not a punishment, nor does it indicate lack of faith. On the contrary, weak ones like you must live by faith, depending on Me to get you through the day. I am developing your ability to trust Me, to lean on Me, rather than on your understanding. Your natural preference is to plan out your day, knowing what will happen when. My preference is for you to depend on Me continually, trusting Me to guide you and strengthen you as needed. This is how you grow strong in your weakness."

~ This devotional, a gift from a friend, as our journey began has not failed to have the words we need to hear each day. Each day has become increasingly more difficult to walk through but I will read Jesus Calling periodically throughout the day to remind me of the words and the strength I received as I read them earlier in the day. Today is no exception.

Today we have not received word about Loren's blood counts, but yesterday they remained bottomed out and he received transfusions again. It was explained to me on Friday that they try to hold off as long as possible to do the transfusions because if he receives too many he could develop antibodies which would make it more difficult to match him for the transfusions he may need. He felt better yesterday and feels good this morning. Friday he was feeling quite weak. He continues to receive many bags of antibiotics in hopes that he won't develop any other infections other than the C-diff bacterial infection they determined he has earlier in the week.

Please continue to pray for Loren's blood counts to go up and for him to remain strong in his faith as we continue along this journey.

~ Praising our Father in Heaven....all in HIS time!

We just heard from the doctor who is on call this weekend...he said, "The white counts are going up"... not a huge amount, but in the right direction! The counts are the highest they have been in a week, so we are PRAISING God, holding fast to God's ability to heal. The sun is up, it is a new day, and we are thankful for this news!

SEPTEMBER 2014

September 1, 2014

Hebrews 10:23
"Let us hold unswervingly to the hope we profess, for he who promised is faithful."

~ Today's devotion in Jesus Calling was a wonderful reminder to me that HE is here, HE knows, and HE is guiding our footsteps through this journey...

Holding on to hope...we continue to do so and this morning we had some really good...and then some not so good news...white cell count continues to creep up! Biggest jump in a week! PRAISING GOD! The not so good news, his platelets dropped again....not sure how or why, but we will continue to pray...

*****

Proverbs 11:25
"The generous will prosper; those who refresh others will themselves be refreshed."

~ Today I received a phone call from a precious friend I have known forever. She asked if she and her husband could meet me before I went up to see Loren in the hospital. The most unexpected thing happened and I was speechless and overcome with emotion. In that moment they were full of God's word and telling me what I have heard several times in the past couple of weeks...that I needed to "learn to receive", and that nothing else need be said but "thank you". I am trying hard to do that, but I needed to share this with my friends and family as it is my way of showing my gratitude for the many blessings Loren and I have been shown in these past months since his illness. I want you both to know that Loren and I will be lifting you up in prayer and Thanksgiving for your love, care, kindness and generosity.

September 2, 2014

Matthew 11:28
""Come to me, all you who are weary and burdened, and I will give you rest."

~ Loren is home...Praise God from Whom All Blessings Flow!

He is tired, he is weary, but he is home. He had an incredible dinner cooked by a dear friend. It is the most I have seen him eat in 10 days...actually longer than that, as he had never actually recovered from his last chemo treatment where he had not been eating much of anything. He took a nice relaxing bath and now he is laying here in our own bed and he is praying. Pray without ceasing...his faith astounds me. It doesn't matter that he is extremely fatigued, he remains steadfast in prayer. While I have struggled in my faith and in darkness I know he has laid there praying not just for his own healing but for me that I continue to find strength and faith to walk this journey with him. His body may be frail, but his faith continues to sustain him.

I pray and ask you all to continue to pray for God to give him rest, to strengthen him and most of all to heal him. Now I will join him in prayer...the devil and his darkness despises this household...he tries really hard to insinuate himself here, but he is up against a true warrior. Let us continue the journey.

September 5, 2014

~ For four years now I have shared over and over again how blessed I feel to be part of the school I work at. I have never realized it more than I have recently. Loren and I have been prayed for, loved, supported, helped, and fed by these extraordinary people. I will never be able to thank all of them enough for all that they have done and will do for us as this journey continues and we continue to need them. Please know how much it means my "family"...more than you will ever know. I love you all!

September 7, 2014

Romans 15:13
"May the God of hope fill you with all joy and peace as you trust in him, so that you may overflow with hope by the power of the Holy Spirit."

~ It has been a wonderful weekend. Loren's family came into town late Friday night and we have sat for the last two days sharing stories, love and prayers together.

Tomorrow Loren will begin what we hope and pray will be a new direction in this journey. He will have an MRI, not just to see what the new chemotherapy has accomplished...and we pray that it is A LOT...but to also map out the gamma knife radiation treatment we are hopeful will happen. We will know more as the week progresses on that matter. The chemo that was used this last treatment was very aggressive and ravaged Loren's body, but not his spirit or faith. This morning he woke up and he finally had color back in his face and a bigger smile on his face than he has had for quite some days. I'm certain it has done wonders for him having the love of his family around him and I am so thankful that they all took the time to come. I can see the difference in him.

I ask you all to continue your prayers to our Father in Heaven. We know that through HIM ALL THINGS ARE POSSIBLE and that tomorrow or Tuesday we will be a witness to HIS healing hand.

Our thanks to ALL of you for EVERYTHING...mostly your prayers and love through this journey!

September 8, 2014

Psalm 59:17
"You are my strength, I sing praise to you; You God are my fortress, my God on whom I can rely."

~ Dear God, you ARE our strength, we have sung your PRAISE and will CONTINUE to do so! Loren has stayed strong in his faith in YOU, he has shown me what it is to be unwavering and although my faith has not been as strong as his through the many prayers of family and dear friends I have found my strength in YOU time and again!

PRAISING YOU GOD FOR YOUR GOODNESS AND MERCY!

Today we have received the most unbelievable news...on two fronts. Loren went for an MRI today for two reasons. First, to see what progress the chemo had made on the cancer, and second to map out the gamma knife radiation treatment.

We had not expected to hear anything today as we have an appointment with the radiology oncologist tomorrow and thought that we would hear everything then. To our surprise, Dr. Dunbar, Loren's oncologist, called shortly after we returned home! I could tell from her voice immediately that she was happy and excited about what had been seen on the scans.

We had NO IDEA! She said, "GREAT NEWS! HUGE IMPROVEMENT was seen on the images!" But we had NO IDEA just what that improvement was. We had never seen the images from when Loren ended up back in the ER before his last chemo when it was found he had a recurrence. Dr. Dunbar informed us today that he had a "lime size" tumor that had developed which has now become the size of a "bean"! PRAISE GOD FROM WHOM ALL BLESSINGS FLOW! And the other tumors are essentially gone! Also, at this time they are putting the radiation on hold, but are still discussing it with us just to make us aware of all of the possibilities.

ALL PRAISE AND GLORY TO OUR FATHER!

HE has heard our unceasing prayers and is working HIS miracle of healing in Loren! And so we pray..."Father please continue to do so. Please continue to strengthen his body so he can continue to fight, please guard his heart and soul from the darkness that at times wants to overtake us both and to YOU WE GIVE GLORY, THANKS AND PRAISE for we know it is YOU we can rely on!"

We love ALL of you and we know that God is hearing all of your prayers that you continue to lift up to HIM on Loren's and our family's behalf. Please continue to do so!

September 10, 2014

~ I have been noticing a lot of posts in the past week about "being thankful." While I have tried to express often to our family and friends who have shown us so much love and support during this time I felt compelled after seeing these posts to take a moment and publicly say how much we love ALL of you for ALL that you have done in these past months. I was told the other day by a sweet friend when I handed her a thank you note that no one expects me to do that. Maybe not, but we have received so many gifts in many different forms and I so wanted to express our gratitude and thanks to you. God Bless all of you!

September 14, 2014

~ "Trust in HIS Spirit"...This morning we attended Mass for the first time in several weeks. It was wonderful to be "home" with our church family to worship our God in whom we have great trust in all circumstances. During Mass Loren had a fainting spell. Scary and disheartening. In a few minutes he was fine. All I could do was say over and over again in my head for the rest of Mass was "Jesus you are our strength and our life. Jesus you are our strength and our life." God, transform us when we are weak and scared.

Tomorrow Loren will go back to the hospital and begin another chemo treatment. I ask myself, was what happened today another test from the darkness that wants to overtake us? In the last few days my head has turned to those hours a few weeks ago that were extremely serious when Loren collapsed and ended up in the ER. I can't shake the wandering of my mind to "what next?" "NO!" "Jesus you are our strength and our life. Jesus you are our strength and our life." BE GONE DARKNESS and ALL YOUR EVIL WAYS! Our trust is in OUR LORD! YOU WILL BE BY LOREN'S SIDE AS HE WALKS THROUGH THIS NEXT JOURNEY!

Pray, pray, pray, for that strength that Loren needs. For God's AWESOME HEALING HAND and for the instruments of healing HE has placed in Loren's life. Pray for them to be filled with HIS wisdom and compassion as Loren goes through this next treatment.

Love to you all.

*****

~ Loren is spending some much needed time with our little grandson. Rest and rejuvenation in preparation for more chemo.

September 15, 2014

~ Loren is beginning another round of chemo today. This treatment marks the first time that Loren will be undergoing treatment without me by his side since the beginning of his diagnosis. It was a difficult decision to make, but the hospital is in Atlanta a half an hour away and the school year and my new position have barely gotten under way. I am feeling very thankful for modern technology and the ability to talk with Loren whenever I want via FaceTime. I choked back tears as my son left with Loren this morning heading into Atlanta.

September 16, 2014

~ It is my birthday. My friends at school made it a special day. I miss my sweetheart who always made it a special day for me...today he completely forgot. Lately he often doesn't even remember what day of the week it is never mind the date.

September 17, 2014

~ Autumn...it is right around the corner. It's a time when strangely, as leaves are turning color, ready to be their most beautiful only to fall from the trees to leave everything barren and brown, I find I am feeling my most refreshed and renewed. It has always been my most favorite time of the year.

Yesterday I left work late and drove to the shopping center in town to do a couple of errands. It was late afternoon and the sun was sitting low in the sky behind a few dark clouds casting a beautiful light on the trees lining the parkway. The tops of the trees are just beginning to show a pale yellow in the right light.

For a moment, just a moment, I was transported to a time when there was no anxiety, no fear, none of the "unknown" that Loren and I have been facing in the past five months. It was a feeling I haven't known for quite some time. If there can be such a thing as a "feeling of hope", I think I felt it...for a few seconds. Memories came flooding back to me. A time when I can remember feeling renewed and refreshed. A time in 1978 when I first met Loren and how in just a few days' time spent with him I knew this was the man I would spend my life with.

Next month we will be married thirty-four years. It is not enough. Thirty-four years is not enough time with a man who has so much more to give to me, to his children, and to his grandchildren.

So today I ask you to pray that God continue to give Loren strength and HOPE to continue his journey, and bring him to complete health once again. Because I am being completely selfish. I want MORE than thirty-four years with this man.

September 19, 2014

~ I received a message from a precious friend who shares that she is "struggling" this morning. Our humanness brings us all "struggles"...to varying degrees. We ALL have struggles in one form or another. May our God who is the ONLY ONE who truly understands the degree of each of our struggles bring us the PEACE that ONLY HE CAN. Love to you all this day.

*****

Psalm 56:3
"When I am afraid I put my trust in You."

~ "I put my trust in YOU." Loren has been in the hospital all week receiving another round of chemo. It has been, for lack of a better word, an odd week. A week filled with many different emotions. Our son and daughter-in-law came over the weekend and stayed with us so that they could drive Loren into Atlanta for his treatment so that I could go to work. When they left, actually before they left, I was filled with sadness. I had been fortunate to be able to spend almost all of Loren's hospital stays with him from the time he was diagnosed until I went back to work at the end of July. Although doing so was often exhausting, I wanted to be by his side. Having him leave on Monday without me was almost too much, given what had happened just a few weeks before which sent him to the hospital for ten days. "I put my trust in YOU"...

Since Loren collapsed a few weeks ago I have found myself sleeping as if I have a newborn once again. I sleep very lightly and awaken with every movement or when I know he is getting out of bed. Any possibility of a stumble sends me reeling out of the bed. So to say that I have gone to bed each night this week and literally passed out while Loren is in the hospital is an understatement. I suppose my mind and my heart is at ease knowing that he is being taken care of by some of the most incredible nurses. Every single one of them there has been nothing but loving, supportive and exceptional at what they do. Knowing that he is in good hands allows me to get the rest I need to continue on this journey with him. Prayer most of all is what has gotten me through this week. Lying in bed each night praying the rosary and letting God know how much I trust in HIM.

Loren's chemo treatment has gone well. Dr. Dunbar has made changes in his chemo treatment this round in hopes that his body will not react the way that it did before. As he nears the end of this treatment though, those fears want to start creeping in once again. "I put my trust in YOU"....

Please pray that Loren's body holds up. That he regains his strength quickly and that the doctors and the knowledge that they are sharing with one another about Loren's treatment is being BLESSED by our Father in Heaven. "I put my trust in YOU."

September 20, 2014

~ The expectation was that Loren would be coming home today. His red blood count dropped and he is beginning to feel weak and so the doctor has decided to keep him in the hospital and give him a transfusion. I have never been known for my patience in regard to anything, but our journey has been a lesson in it for me. I'm still not very good at it. But, there is Loren. He's lying there making it a guy thing. Football is on...yes, there's always football! It's a gorgeous, nearly autumn afternoon, and I've spent the day doing all of those mundane, but oh so necessary things...bank, drug store, grocery shopping....putting groceries away and now I will put together some meals for the week. These are the times when this life, this journey we have been on for months now, is difficult. These are the things we always have done together but now I do them alone because even when he is not in the hospital he is either too tired, too weak, or we feel he shouldn't be out and about for fear that he will get sick because of his lowered immune system.

But, I am practicing "patience"...I ask God nearly every moment of every day to help me realize that it is "all in HIS timing"...I believe our life will continue to be filled with the mundane...but we will do it TOGETHER!... PRAYERS!

September 21, 2014

Psalm 5:3
"In the morning Lord, you hear my voice; In the morning, I lay my requests before you and wait expectantly."

~ Loren is feeling well this morning and is waiting for the doctor to come to his room...praying his counts have improved so he can come home on this beautiful Sunday...maybe he will feel well enough to sit on the back porch and soak in this beautiful first day of Autumn...praying.

*****

~ Loren is coming home! Follow up lab work tomorrow of course to check his counts, but he will be in the comfort of his own home!

Today was another day that I have been reminded of how amazingly kind and loving people's hearts are....and how, as my sister reminded me, God is at work in our lives, most especially at this difficult time. I thank her for reminding me of that. After all this time I shouldn't have to be reminded, I'm sad that I had to be. Sometimes I suppose I let the sadness and the gravity of our situation rule my heart and mind, rather than be open to the fact that GOD IS ALWAYS HERE. HE is working through others in our lives.

Because Loren didn't come home yesterday the "plans for the day" got a little discombobulated. I had to find someone to go get Loren at the hospital. I no sooner began thinking about a solution to how Loren was coming home from the hospital when a certain person popped into my head. When I say that literally not even a minute later the phone rang and it was him, I am not kidding! GOD AT WORK! His first question was, "What can I do for you?" I told him what was happening and that I was going to need to find someone to pick Loren up at the hospital. He said, "I will be happy to help with that." GOD AT WORK!

Earlier in the day one of our neighbors stopped in. She handed me a card, visited a few minutes and left. An extremely thoughtful gift was inside...not expected, but certainly needed and appreciated so deeply. GOD AT WORK!

Through this entire time we have had so many unbelievable and so very thoughtful things given to us. I would be remiss if I didn't mention our other neighbors. They have been so giving and supportive. They have helped the entire summer with our lawn, with helping to get us places when I had days I felt I just couldn't do it, and preparing numerous meals for us after long stays in the hospital.

For all of you that so many times have sent messages, given hugs and the endless prayers...we don't know what the future holds, but we know we don't have to face it alone.

I never realized how truly blessed we are and my gratefulness is overflowing.

...and Papa is being loved and cared for by his little man. No better medicine than that!

September 22, 2014

Hebrews 10:23
"Let us hold unswervingly to the hope we profess, for He who promised is faithful."

Jesus Calling ~
"Trust Me and refuse to worry, for I am your Strength and Song. You are feeling wobbly this morning, looking at difficult times looming ahead, measuring them against your own strength. However, they are not today's tasks— or even tomorrow's. So leave them in the future and come home to the present, where you will find Me waiting for you. Since I am your Strength, I can empower you to handle each task as it comes. Because I am your Song, I can give you Joy as you work alongside Me.
Keep bringing your mind back to the present moment. Among all My creatures, only humans can anticipate future events. This ability is a blessing, but it becomes a curse whenever it is misused. If you use your magnificent mind to worry about tomorrow, you cloak yourself in dark unbelief. However, when the hope of heaven fills your thoughts, the Light of My Presence envelops you.

Though heaven is future, it is also present tense. As you walk in the Light with Me, you have one foot on earth and one foot in heaven."

~ Today's devotion in Jesus Calling brings me peace.

September 24, 2014

~ "Hope"... Some days I wonder what that really is. Each day I leave the house being "hopeful" that it will be a better day for Loren. This chemo that he has been going through these past couple of times is knocking the wind out of him. He has had a rough couple of days and we are once again in the ER.

Besides that, we had someone who was doing a good deed for us and through some very unfortunate turn of events, ended up with her car barreling down our driveway and damaging our garage and possibly the foundation on that end of our house.

I was telling some co-workers at the end of the day today in a short-lived teary moment, that "I just wanted our life back". Please don't take this comment as a complaint. It is a heartfelt sadness of the way our life used to be. We have never lived our life extravagantly. It has never been a life full of excitement. But certainly enough good times for us to consider ourselves "happy" and "blessed". I just truly miss those moments of just being able to say, "Hey, let's go get a bite to eat" or "Let's go hang out at Target or Lowe's" or somewhere other than a hospital room or ER or even just the family room in our house.

I made a comment on Facebook over the past week and received some comments saying I am "lucky" for this, that and the other thing. They were comments that stung. Sometimes I think people don't stop and think before they make comments...about how they could be received by the person reading them. Perhaps they weren't meant that way, but the power of the written word can be easily misconstrued. I know this in a very personal way.

My husband has brain cancer....those are pretty powerful words. Our life has been forever changed by this journey...those are pretty powerful words. We don't know what God's will is in this situation...those are pretty powerful words, and from my very soul, I just want our life back...THOSE are the most powerful words of all.

If you don't understand those feelings after what we have been experiencing over the past five to six months, I just don't even know what to say to that, but what you need to know is that this is NOT a complaint, it is life, and it is our life that has been shaken to its core.

I am "hopeful" that Loren will be going home tonight and not have to be admitted into the hospital once again...and tomorrow HOPE will allow us try all over again.

September 25, 2014

~ They are admitting Loren to the hospital. His white cell count has dramatically dropped once again and his platelets are very low as well. Not sure what the game plan is at this point, just that he is being admitted.

September 27, 2014

Proverbs 30:5
"Every word of God is pure; HE is a shield onto them that put their trust in HIM."

~ For my precious husband...so today did not turn out the way we had hoped, but we continue to place our trust in God. We "are not on a journey to God, but on a journey WITH God." HE has been with us every step of the way. HE has placed people in our lives who with HIM and with the abilities HE has given them are keeping you as strong and as healthy as you can be. Hold onto that, hold onto your faith in HIM. HE is walking with you, carrying you when need to be carried, and comforting you always.

Yesterday we had been told that Loren would probably be discharged from the hospital today. After several transfusions since Wednesday his counts still are not rebounding. The oncologist saw him a short while ago and said that he is concerned that Loren's body is not doing the job on its own. For safety sake they are keeping him here in the hospital so that he does not risk getting an infection. Disappointing for certain, but if Loren's chemo treatments do what they are supposed to do then we want the best supportive care he can get so that he has a fighting chance to be well again.

September 28, 2014

James 4:7
"Submit yourselves therefore to God. Resist the devil, and
he will flee from you."

Jesus Calling ~
"Open your mind and heart—your entire being—to
receive My Love in full measure. So many of My children
limp through their lives starved for Love, because they
haven't learned the art of receiving. This is essentially an
act of faith: believing that I love you with boundless,
everlasting Love. The art of receiving is also a discipline:
training your mind to trust Me, coming close to Me with
confidence. Remember that the evil one is the father of
lies. Learn to recognize his deceptive intrusions into your
thoughts. One of his favorite deceptions is to undermine
your confidence in My unconditional Love. Fight back
against these lies! Do not let them go unchallenged. Resist
the devil in My Name, and he will slink away from you.
Draw near to Me, and My Presence will envelop you in
Love.
I pray that out of his glorious riches he may strengthen
you with power through his Spirit in your inner being, so
that Christ may dwell in your hearts through faith. And I
pray that you, being rooted and established in love, may
have power, together with all the saints, to grasp how
wide and long and high and deep is the love of Christ."

~ The darkness has worked overtime in these last
five months...it is hard each day to resist...it takes A LOT
of energy to "submit myself" each day to God. Darkness

is powerful...but HE, THE ALMIGHTY is FAR MORE POWERFUL. I'll show it, I'll show it... Today's Jesus Calling devotion...YES!

September 28, 2014

~ For my precious husband, I've stayed in love with you all these years because of the million tiny things you've continued to do all these years...

September 30, 2014

Matthew 6:34
"Do not worry about tomorrow, for tomorrow will bring worries of its own. Today's trouble is enough for today."

Jesus Calling ~
"I am perpetually with you, taking care of you. That is the most important fact of your existence. I am not limited by time or space; My Presence with you is a forever-promise. You need not fear the future, for I am already there. When you make that quantum leap into eternity, you will find Me awaiting you in heaven. Your future is in My hands; I release it to you day by day, moment by moment. Therefore, do not worry about tomorrow. I want you to live this day abundantly, seeing all there is to see, doing all there is to do. Don't be distracted by future concerns. Leave them to Me! Each day of life is a glorious gift, but so few people know how to live within the confines of today. Much of their energy for abundant living spills over the time line into tomorrow's worries or past regrets. Their remaining energy is sufficient only for

limping through the day, not for living it to the full. I am training you to keep your focus on My Presence in the present. This is how to receive abundant Life, which flows freely from My throne of grace."

~ Each day, one step at a time...I'm trying Lord, I'm trying.

Loren remains in the hospital. His counts actually dropped a bit yesterday and while I was with him he received another transfusion of platelets. We try to remember, "All in HIS time, ALL in HIS time"...I am lifted up by today's devotion.

OCTOBER 2014

October 1, 2014

Psalm 119:28
"My soul is weary with sorrow; strengthen me according to your word."

~ The last few days my body and mind has known a weariness it has never known before. The sorrow of the past six months I feel is starting to takes its toll. I'm not sure I have ever felt this fatigued before. I made myself a doctor appointment and of course, when I went besides wanting to run a ton of blood work the easy fix is "why don't we give you a little something"...I'm not sure they get it. "A little something" isn't going to "fix" anything. It will mask it all, only to be dealt with later on. What I rely on is the strength and the power of the only true healer, for both myself and for Loren. Rest, rest is what my soul and my body needs...and so it is 9PM and I will give myself the rest I need.

Today Loren's white count went up. Just a bit, but a trend upward, so we will take it. Praise God! The doctor says the platelets should start following suit. Loren has run a low grade fever for a few days which has broken, another positive thing, especially since they couldn't pin point the reason for the fever.

Oh Lord, "Strengthen us according to your word"...

October 2, 2014

~ Today our second grandson was born. Surely a time that should be full of joy, but Papa is still in the hospital. Our family lives 45 minutes away and I want to go spend time with them. I do not want to go without Loren, but I want to see our new grandson. I leave with a heavy heart to go to them, but there is a precious new life to greet. Precious and beautiful.

October 4, 2014

Ephesians 5:20
"Giving thanks always and for everything to God the Father in the name of our Lord Jesus Christ."

~ ...in ALL things. This morning I am giving thanks for our little grandson, a beautiful gift from God, healthy and precious in every way. Giving thanks for this beautiful autumn day that has me filled with a renewed spirit. Even giving thanks for this journey that Loren and I have been on, difficult as it has been, physically, emotionally and spiritually. Through it all I have become closer to God. I am developing the relationship I have always wanted to have with our Father...in ALL things give THANKS!

October 5, 2014

~ Today I did something I haven't done in several months. I went to Target. Yup, went to Target. The first time I have been in a store other than to pick up groceries or medications in months. The last time I was there I was with Loren. He was going through his methotrexate chemotherapy and was in between chemo sessions. He was feeling pretty good then. We had been to the hospital for labs and had gotten a bite to eat and then we decided to walk around Target for a little bit. For most everyone that is no big deal. There was a time we thought nothing about just getting in the car and hanging out somewhere. Now we can't. Now Loren spends most of his time in the hospital and when he is out of the hospital his immune system is so suppressed it is dangerous for him to be anywhere but at home.

Our daughter and son-in-law have been deployed for several months now and I haven't sent them the first little care package since they have been away. I feel so badly about that. I feel as though I am neglecting so many things in our lives. So today I decided to go to the store and put a few things together for them so I can ship a package to them. For just a little while it felt "normal" to be out and about. But so many times while I was out my thoughts turned to Loren and I would look at my watch and think, "I have to finish and get back to Loren." So many times I wished he was there walking beside me helping me to decide, "Should I send this or that?" So many times I longed for our life to be the way it used to be, and so many times I felt the sadness try to overtake me. It's funny how just the simplest of things now can evoke such emotion in me. Nothing seems right, nothing.

Today Loren was told by the doctor that he will most likely remain in the hospital until at least Monday. Today is day ten. Each day I come to the hospital my heart aches to see what this cancer and the treatment has done to his body. I want to scream out "THIS ISN'T FAIR!" But I realize that life isn't fair for so many.

Please continue to remember Loren in prayer. Time goes on, life goes on, but our life continues on this journey and we need your continued love, support and prayers to strengthen us along the way.

*****

~ One thing I know for sure is that this journey we are on is an ever winding road, with twists and turns and road blocks. After being told yesterday that he would probably not be home until tomorrow at the earliest, Loren was told this morning that it is very possible he could be discharged today, albeit late. He wants to come home. He's had enough, we both have. His white cell count nearly doubled over night but his platelets are still low and they were transfusing him again today as well as giving him IV potassium and more antibiotics. Having been told that, I told him that I wanted to stay home here and get the house ready for him....to "clean". I have spent the day doing this and have stopped to rest and have a cup of coffee. Although I am happy Loren is coming home I have been filled with sadness and grief, for so many reasons.

"Cleaning"...I have come to the realization while doing it today that it has been as much for my soul as it has been to "clean" the house. Once again a day where I am all too aware of the big picture. The aloneness and the grief that washes over me as I "clean"... the "things" that I have dealt with and the "things" I have not.

I was dusting in the living room. On the console table is a photo of my Dad that I put together after his death June 17th along with the "Peace of Mind" picture that some of you may remember has deep meaning for our family. My soul realized at that moment that I have not even begun to grieve for my father. There is a lot to grieve... and I don't even know how it is going to be possible, because there is so much to grieve for right now in mine and Loren's life.

I am thankful for the moments that I allow myself to shed sacred tears. When I do, I feel stronger. I am thankful for those who allow me to shed sacred tears with them. When I do, it strengthens me. The tears are how I share my overwhelming grief, whether I am aware of it or not.

So now, I will continue to "clean" as much for my soul, as to welcome Loren home. Maybe somehow my tears will be a "cleansing", much like when you have your home "blessed" and Loren will feel loved and comforted much like I do when I allow myself "sacred tears".

*****

~ It is late and he is HOME! Praying God gives him a peaceful night's rest in the comfort of his own bed.

October 8, 2014

Psalm 39:7
"And so, Lord, where do I put my hope? My only hope is in you."

~ As this day comes to a close ours has ended with a second phone call to the oncologist that has been taking care of Loren's emergency care here on the south side of town so as to not have to travel to Atlanta to get the care he might need. Ever since he was in the hospital for 11 days he has run a fever. It has been anywhere from 99 to the highest of 101.2. We were told the "magic number" is 100.5. So as you might imagine, we have been quite concerned. Most especially since no one can seem to tell us why this is happening. About a half an hour ago I spoke with one of the oncologists who I haven't really had a favorable opinion of...up until tonight. He literally spent a half an hour on the phone with me sharing different theories of why this could be happening and going back over Loren's hospital stay and the decisions that were made very thoroughly. I was impressed to say the least. But it was what he told me about my husband that impressed me the most. Once again I am reminded of what an extraordinary man I am married to and how extraordinary his faith is. It has to be, I truly believe after my conversation with the doctor tonight that his faith is the ONLY thing which has brought him this far in this journey. The doctor told me that the type of chemo and amount that he has been given, which has completely ravaged his body, that Loren has journeyed 10 miles farther than most anyone he has known. That being said, he also said that Loren cannot continue to have this kind of treatment at this level. He cannot continue to have his bone marrow wiped out the way that it has been. I'm not sure about anything right now except for the fact that Loren's faith and the unceasing prayers of our circle of family and friends have kept him strong...mind, body and spirit. I ask you PLEASE DO NOT STOP! I am convinced now more than ever that miracles DO happen, I believe I have one laying here beside me right now. God bless my precious husband and give him the strength he needs to keep fighting!

October 11, 2014

~ Today I am married to this man for thirty-four years. To be honest, there have been days in the past six months that I feared we would not make it to today, especially in the last month. The vows we took on this day thirty-four years ago have always meant a lot to us, but never as meaningful as they have been right now. "In sickness and in health"... words at twenty years old don't have the depth of meaning that they do right now and the journey we have been facing since April 19th of this year.

Usually around this time we have had discussions of a weekend get-a-way to celebrate our special day or about where we would like to have dinner. Today we are happy just to be out of the hospital and to be together to watch college football. Cherish every moment. If there is one lesson I have learned through this journey that I don't feel I did often enough in the past thirty-four years, it is to cherish every moment. Even those that aren't full of excitement or necessarily joyful.

So today I sit here thankful that God has given us this day to cherish and to celebrate just being here together. Happy Anniversary my precious husband.

*****

~ Anniversary dinner...today was full of those cherished moments...sitting around watching football all day...the DAWGS ruled, the JACKETS got beat, and we had a cup of coffee together. To most a cup of coffee together is no big deal. For us it is. It's one of those things we enjoyed nearly every afternoon together when home from work. Since his treatments he has had no taste for it. Today he said, "I think I might like a cup of coffee with you," and he seemed to enjoy the taste of it. We even shared some popcorn while watching football. Such little things, but things missed and now cherished, most especially today. Dinner was Olive Garden that I picked up and brought home and tried to make as special as one could given the circumstances. I think it was even better than going to the restaurant. A day full of cherished moments, indeed...

October 12, 2014

Matthew 6:25-27
"Therefore I tell you, do not worry about your life, what you will eat or drink; or about your body, what you will wear. Is life not more than food, and the body more than clothes? Look at the birds of the air; they do not sow or reap or store away in barns, and yet your heavenly Father feeds them. Are you not much more valuable than they? Can any one of you by worrying add a single hour to your life"?

~ These few scripture verses have become a favorite of mine in these last months, and it has been an exercise in faith to "not worry" but to be prayerful about ALL of the concerns we have had in the last six months. Loren's health of course is at the top of the list. Strength of mind, body and spirit for both of us and of course our home and finances would follow. In ALL of these things God has continued to show his presence to us by placing in our lives at the moments we have had the most concern his loving instruments in the form of family and friends who have been here EVERY step of the way through this journey. We are so thankful for every opportunity to see his loving presence in our lives.

Tomorrow Loren will have an MRI. I have done my best to push this scan out of my mind this weekend. As the day is beginning to draw to an end it has moved front and center in my thoughts. I am doing my absolute best to "not worry", but to offer a prayer every time it creeps into my thoughts. Prayers of thanksgiving as his last MRI had such phenomenal results and prayers of healing that God has continued to work his miracle of healing in Loren.

So, I am asking you to continue to walk this journey with us and continue to keep Loren in prayer.

October 13, 2014

Proverbs 3: 5-6
"Trust in the Lord with all your heart, and lean not on your own understanding; in all your ways acknowledge him, and he shall direct your paths."

~ Once again God shows us that HE is right here walking this journey with us. At 8:30 this morning Loren went for his bloodwork to once again check his counts. HUGE jumps in his counts! His red cells dropped just a little bit so he remains anemic, but that is to be expected while undergoing chemo. His white cell count is high enough so he is not as prone to infection! PRAISE GOD! On to the MRI...GOD HAS CONTINUED TO WORK HIS WONDROUS MIRACLE OF HEALING IN LOREN! Dr. Dunbar called barely 15 minutes after we left the hospital to tell us there was significant improvement in Loren's scan since the last one! She says she is so happy with the scan that she is in no hurry to bring him in for a treatment right away which is going to give him time to regain strength in his body and for his counts to continue to improve! PRAISE GOD, PRAISE GOD, PRAISE GOD! I now know that those are two words that can NEVER be said enough! Let them ALWAYS be on my lips Lord!

Thank you to EVERY SINGLE ONE OF YOU that continues to lift Loren in prayer to our Father in Heaven, and thank you for EVERYTHING you do to love, care and support us....the journey continues....

October 14, 2014

James 1: 2-4
"Consider it pure joy, whenever you face trials of many kinds, because you know that the testing of your faith produces perseverance. Let perseverance finish its work so that you may be mature and complete, not lacking anything."

~ So many times in the past six months this very thought has occurred to me. That it is through this suffering, both Loren's physical and our emotional suffering, that our faith has been tested over and over again and we continue to persevere. We continue to fight against the darkness that wants us to give up on our God. It wants us to find fault with HIM because of what we are experiencing. But every day, and I do mean EVERY day, there is something no matter how small to find true JOY in. Yesterday there was much to be JOYFUL about; once again our God has proven to us that we will persevere in this tough time. We don't know what the outcome will be, but we will stay JOYFUL along this journey. Finding joy in the smallest of things, a hug or a smile or a laugh along the way. A cup of coffee, sitting at the table enjoying a meal together...these are the things we are finding joy in. Praying our God continues to allow us to do this together.

October 23, 2014

Psalm 23:4
"Even though I walk through the darkest valley, I will fear no evil, for you are with me; your rod and your staff, they comfort me."

~ How do you go from such joy to such angst in no time at all? This is our journey from day to day, sometimes from hour to hour....and this is the Psalm, the prayer that Loren has said non-stop for the past six months over and over again. It was mine through the night. We were reminded once again that our God is with us always, most especially when we walk through the darkest valleys or hours, and because we are human we fear the evil that works constantly to overtake us.

It has been MY belief for years that "the evil one" works overtime on my husband because his faith is so deep. Loren has suffered with anxiety and nightmares for years. They haven't increased during the last six months but they have become more vivid. Last night was a good example of that. God was preparing me for this last night. I rarely go to bed early, but last night I was in bed by 8:30. Around 12:30 this morning I was awakened by the most horrendous sound. The same one that I heard the morning Loren collapsed on his way to the bathroom. This time, he was right next to the bed. I jumped out of the bed to his side with the same words (he reminded me) that I said the last time, "Dear God, what happened?!" He had been having a nightmare. He said, "I was back on the farm and was falling down the hay chute and when I hit the bottom I rolled so the hay wouldn't fall on me." He literally rolled in his sleep and rolled right off of the bed, hitting his head on the nightstand. Praise God he was not injured! I got him up and into the bathroom so I could check him out. Then the darkness wanted to take over. Loren said it. He said, "The last time I was having dreams like this the cancer had grown"...yes, but he had also been exhibiting other symptoms as well. Here's my take, we had an incredible evening of joy and hope, lots of wonderful conversation about how well he is feeling and hopeful for the future. So, the evil one decided to intervene. Psalm 23, Loren's prayer, but mine as well last night. God had prepared me by prodding me to go to sleep early because from 12:30 until my alarm went off at 5AM, there was not much sleep. Psalm 23, "thy rod and thy staff, they comfort me"...all through the night. WE WILL NOT GIVE INTO THE FEAR THAT DARKNESS WANTS US TO!

Continued prayers, that Loren be healed by our Lord and Savior and that as we move into this new phase of disability for Loren we take comfort in our Lord walking this journey with us, helping us physically, emotionally, spiritually, and financially.

October 25, 2014

~ Life has become, for lack of a better word, interesting. Each day begins with searching for that reason to find JOY in each day, and each day I realize that I don't have to look any further than the man lying in the bed next to me. The JOY that God has given me yet another day to have him in my life. That is my JOY considering our journey in the past six months.

We invited friends for dinner tonight. Amazing how something as common as inviting someone for dinner feels as if your life is "normal" again. "Normal"...we wondered the other night if our life would ever be "normal" again? No day ever seems to go by without being planned out...lots of planning. But what JOY we had while sitting for several hours sharing wine, (really good wine), good food and good conversation....simple, but joyful moments.

Praying for more days, more evenings of these simple but joyful experiences that are so often taken for granted, but today for us, were the things that helped turn pain into joy in the present grief.

October 26, 2014

John 15:5
"I am the vine; you are the branches. If a man remains in me and I in him, he will bear much fruit; apart from me you can do nothing."

Jesus Calling ~
"Come to Me when you are hurting, and I will soothe your pain. Come to Me when you are joyful, and I will share your Joy, multiplying it many times over. I am All you need, just when you need it. Your deepest desires find fulfillment in Me alone.
This is the age of self-help. Bookstores abound with books about "taking care of number one," making oneself the center of all things. The main goal of these methodologies is to become self-sufficient and confident. You, however, have been called to take a "road less traveled": continual dependence on Me. True confidence comes from knowing you are complete in My Presence. Everything you need has its counterpart in Me."

NOVEMBER 2014

November 4, 2014

~ Awoke to a beautiful sunrise...a reminder that even after the darkest night, GOD IS GOOD and HE is there, all the time.

*****

Exodus 33:14
"The Lord replied, "My presence will go with you, and I will give you rest."

~ Praying our Lord will give Loren and I much needed rest to restore our bodies and our souls.

*****

Psalm 29:11
"The Lord gives strength to His people; The Lord blesses His people with peace."

November 7, 2014

~ I have learned in the last seven months how much I have taken for granted throughout my life, but today I have SO much gratitude. I have said so many times in the past few days, "It's the little things," and it truly is.

Today I raced off after school to the hospital where Loren had been dropped off by a neighbor for a doctor appointment, once again to check his blood counts. We are praising God for once again showing HIS mighty hand and HIS ability to heal. Loren's body continues to grow stronger day by day. The doctor told Loren that he cannot believe how resilient his body is. We, on the other hand, know that it is through the power of prayer and God's healing hand that he has regained his strength and bone marrow. The doctor also shared with Loren just how serious his condition had been in the hospital. Very sobering. We continue to believe in the power of prayer.

While in the doctor office I realized that I had left my iPad sitting on my desk at school. So we drove by the school to pick it up and Loren wanted to come in. He had not been in the school but a few minutes right after the school year started. What a joy it was to show him the colorful, cheerful hallways on "The Hill" and for him to finally meet my co-worker who brings me so much happiness every day, and we stopped throughout the hallways to say hello to a few other special people along the way! Something so simple and taken for granted for all these years, but today this simple thing brings so much gratitude.

Next stop, grocery shopping...the man cannot stop eating! That is really good news! Another chore that I have so missed doing with Loren by my side...grocery shopping. Tooling through Walmart, which frankly I normally despise, but today I am full of gratitude that my six foot one tall husband could reach up and behind the things I usually have a hard time getting myself! Something I always took for granted in the past. Today I am full of gratitude that he is healthy enough to be walking through Walmart to shop with me!

What a day! Full of the "little things" that are often taken for granted, but find me full of gratitude today!

We ask that you continue lifting Loren in prayer. In the next couple of weeks Loren will have another MRI and a few days later we will meet with Dr. Dunbar, his neuro-oncologist, to discuss how to continue Loren's treatment. We were a bit disconcerted today while meeting with the doctor. He looked at us and said, "So you are done with chemotherapy"... that is not a discussion that Dr. Dunbar has had with us at all. It is possible that she has been consulting with him about that. We don't know what other options there are other than radiation. Please continue to pray that God's healing hand has been at work and that chemo does not have to continue and that if radiation is necessary that it does not cause any damage. Loren will also have treatment to prevent a type of pneumonia that can occur in people with a lowered immune system.

This has been an incredibly long journey with so many twists and turn. This week has not been a good week for me emotionally or spiritually. Yes I know it isn't about me, but I am here walking this journey beside Loren and I continue to need your prayers as well. Thank you and God Bless...take nothing for granted and be full of gratitude in all the "little things".

November 12, 2014

~ If there is one thing I have learned about myself in the last seven months it is the depth of my honesty. I feel I have always been an honest person, but through this journey I feel that on most days I have been brutally honest about the difficulty of this journey for both Loren and myself...physically, emotionally and spiritually...and

117

so it goes. In the last couple of weeks although surrounded by people I have felt alone. In the "aloneness" I have shared feelings, brutally honest feelings that perhaps I shouldn't have. You trust that heartfelt feelings are left between two people, most likely they haven't been. If you are offended by hearing of my "feelings"... my "honesty" then I feel for you, and I pray that you might never have to experience what we are experiencing in our life. Until you have walked in my shoes you cannot fathom the pain, the exhaustion, the fear and any number of other emotions that lay just below the surface of a smiling facade. The smile does not make me a fake or a phony. The smile is me knowing that every day is a gift, for me and for my husband and our family, and that God is already there ahead of me each day. My hurt, my pain, my disappointments are in my heart, God knows them, and HE is the only one I need to reconcile them with. Do not judge my heart or my feelings...because none of us knows what our hearts or feelings would be in any given situation, and certainly not this one. God is not judging me, HE is working to heal my hurt and my pain...and I am ready to receive HIS forgiveness.

November 13, 2014

~ Tonight we were able to have a bit of that "quality of life" Loren's doctor so often speaks about. Something we rarely have had the opportunity to partake in these past seven months. We were able to attend our little grandson's "art show" at his preschool.

What a joy to spend time with him while he showed off his "masterpieces" and we were able to watch him participate in singing with his preschool class. What a joy for Loren to be there and for him to be feeling stronger. Praising God for this day!

*****

~ Funny little story! Our son was just telling us that lately our grandson has been saying, "Honey will do it." Or, "I will tell honey"....after a few times our son asked him, "Who is honey?" And he said, "Papa"! Matt asked, "Who calls Papa honey?"...."Lala does"! Oh my goodness! They are always listening aren't they? What joy!

November 14, 2014

~ Today is our grandson's third birthday! Yet another joyful moment to share in! Praising God!

November 16, 2014

Romans 15:13
"May the God of hope fill you with all joy and peace as you trust in Him."

~ The past few days of devotions that I have read have been speaking directly to my mind and my heart and how I have been feeling the past couple of weeks. As we come closer to November 20th when Loren will have his next MRI I find myself becoming more anxious...about everything. Especially on those days when Loren seems to be having a more "forgetful" day. Is it proof of what may be lurking inside his brain? Is it just fatigue, or perhaps the fact that the man is going to be 59 years old soon? Aren't we all allowed some forgetfulness from time to time? When the fear begins to take over I try to remind myself of who is beside me, holding my hand...and that HE is already there, regardless of the outcome of the MRI. This morning we went to Mass. We have missed having our hearts and souls filled with the grace of the Eucharist and certainly the love of the many people who have sustained us with their prayers in these last seven months. After Mass Loren spoke with someone who works at Delta. He asked Loren if he was "going back to work"... Loren said "no"...at first he didn't qualify it by saying, "Not yet"...and it struck a note of fear in me. I wondered if he had decided that life as we know it was how it was going to remain. But a few minutes later he began saying how we weren't sure what direction the doctor was moving in with his treatment. The hopefulness began to return...

As the 20th of November approaches please continue to keep Loren in prayer. God has done wondrous things, the conversation with his doctor last week proves how God has been working in Loren and in me, strengthening us each day. We pray HE is ready to show HIS mighty hand as only HE can when we receive the results of the MRI.

Thank you for all the love, hugs, and prayers today...we are lifted up. God bless!

November 19, 2014

~ Today is exactly seven months since Loren's diagnosis of brain cancer. It has been seven months full of many things, not the least of which is growth in our faith, most especially mine. The last few days Loren and I have been preparing ourselves spiritually and emotionally for tomorrow afternoon. Loren will have an MRI for the first time in several weeks and it has been many weeks since his last chemo treatment. Each time we begin to question what will happen we remind each other that God is already there...as HE has been this entire journey. We already know the ultimate destination of our journey here on earth, as our faith tells us, is to go HOME into HIS presence. So we are confident that HE is there regardless of the outcome tomorrow. Praising God for HIS love and comfort in these past seven months and asking all of you to pray tonight and through tomorrow for God to reveal to us his wondrous healing power. With love.

November 20, 2014

Psalm 62:8
"Trust in Him at all times. Pour out your heart to Him, for God is our refuge."

~ HE is already here...today, tomorrow and always....

Psalm 27:14
"Wait on the Lord; be of good courage, and He shall strengthen thine heart; wait, I say, on the Lord."

~ No word yet on Loren's MRI...we are waiting and being "of good courage"....

November 21, 2014

1 Chronicles 16:8
"Oh give thanks to the Lord, call upon His name; make known His deeds among the peoples."

~ "Give THANKS and MAKE KNOWN HIS DEEDS!" ...and so we will! Thank you God for you ARE GOOD...in ALL things and ALL the time! We heard from Dr. Dunbar this morning! The word is "universally stable" which is such VERY GOOD news! The last time Loren went even just a few weeks without treatment he had a HUGE recurrence. It has been weeks without treatment and there has been virtually no change! This is excellent news! We will meet with Dr. Dunbar on Monday and we will discuss what the next step will be. God is so good, and we want to thank ALL of you who continue to lift your voices to HIM on Loren's behalf...and mine, for not only has Loren continued to stay healthy through this battle, but I have as well. Given where I work, that is NO small miracle in itself! We have MUCH to be thankful for in this beautiful season! We love our God, and we love ALL of you for your continued love, support and prayers!

November 22, 2014

~ With my honey at the table this morning enjoying a cup of coffee and talking to our new grandbaby on FaceTime...it's the "little things"...joyful moments...

November 23, 2014

~ Heading to church this morning with hearts overflowing with THANKFULNESS! First, Loren's news this week and this morning we received a text from our daughter that she and our son-in-law were beginning the final leg of their journey home from their deployment! In fact, they should be landing soon! Thankful for ALL of you who have kept our family in prayer! Love to all!

*****

Psalm 107:22
"And let them offer sacrifices of thanksgiving, and tell of his deeds in songs of joy."

~ Along this long journey I have often been asked "how do I do it?" This is HOW and WHY...THANKING OUR LORD in EVERY situation whether good, or difficult...God's Grace and HIS Grace alone is how...

November 24, 2014

Ephesians 2:8
"For by grace are ye saved through faith; and that not of yourselves: it is the gift of God."

~ Today, once again, we have been reminded of God's Grace in our lives that has been given to us through our faith in HIM.

We met with Dr. Dunbar this morning. It was our first visit with her since July when Loren was diagnosed with the recurrence of lymphoma and started the

123

journey of two chemotherapy sessions that almost took his life. Harsh words but true. I felt it during those days, but it was confirmed by his other oncologist a couple of weeks ago just how serious Loren's condition was.

Today we learned something that I didn't want to hear, but somehow I knew in my heart, and it was only learned because I had the strength to ask the question. Quite bluntly I asked Dr. Dunbar. She was talking with us about how she did "not want to do any treatment right now...things looked good...no reason while Loren is regaining strength to tear his body down" etcetera; etcetera....I didn't like the things I was hearing. Or better yet, what I was not hearing. I told her that I was going to ask her the question that had not been asked. "Was there going to be no cure for Loren?" The look on her face said everything to me.

Dr. Dunbar is no longer looking towards a "curative intent" with Loren. She told us that given how quickly the cancer came back after his initial treatment it was not a good sign, but that being said, Dr. Dunbar is very happy with the fact that he has had several MRI scans that show his condition has remained stable.

I then asked her in her experience what that means for Loren time wise. She said she has had patients live five, ten, fifteen and even twenty years in a "stable" condition with lymphoma like Loren's. Yes, not the news we wanted to hear today, but by our faith we have been given the gift of Grace from God to continue this journey. As I told our pastor this afternoon, "Dr. Dunbar does not have the last word in this." That being said, we want to ask you to please continue your prayers for Loren...and for me. Your prayers have brought us to today, strong of mind, body and spirit and we NEED you to continue them for us. The new year will bring many challenges, of that we are certain. Please keep us in prayer.

November 25, 2014

~ Today I have been reflecting on how thankful Loren and I feel to all of you who have lifted your voices in prayer on his behalf. All of a sudden the scene from the classic movie "It's A Wonderful Life" popped into my head. It is the moment where all the stars in the sky are shown and in the dark of night all the voices of George's family and friends can be heard drifting up towards our Father in Heaven. It's what I imagine it sounds like to our Father in Heaven when your voices reach HIM as you pray for Loren. Please continue your prayers...HE is listening...love and prayers of gratitude to you all!

November 27, 2014

~ Thankful, grateful, blessed to be spending the day together with family. Thanksgiving Day. A day that has so much meaning to us today.

November 28, 2014

~ Family Christmas tree up...feet up...glass of mistletoe for me and my honey..."Home Alone" in the DVR....and all is right with the world...it's the little things in life that we should take joy in...

November 29, 2014

Philippians 3:20–21
"But our citizenship is in heaven. And we eagerly await a
Savior from there, the Lord Jesus Christ, who, by the
power that enables him to bring everything under his
control, will transform our lowly bodies so that they will
be like his glorious body."

~ Tomorrow is the first Sunday of Advent, and although I "eagerly await the Savior from Heaven" I find myself not wanting to move forward in life, even though we are asked to move forward in our spiritual life in preparation for HIS coming. Why move forward to a time of uncertainty? Why move away from a time in our lives where we know Loren is feeling well? We are enjoying every moment, cherishing each moment like we never have before in our lives together. Because we know that "in the waiting" for our Savior, in our preparation, we become aware that HE WAS, HE IS and EVER SHALL BE....HE is here NOW in our present hour of need, and HE IS ALREADY THERE IN OUR FUTURE. This is our belief, and we pray that we will continue to hold that in our heart through this Advent season and HIS glorious coming at Christmas. God bless all of you and please continue praying for Loren and his continued healing and strength.

DECEMBER 2014

~ As December began I started to notice changes in Loren both physically and mentally. He seemed to be struggling once again with balance and his short term memory was beginning to show changes as well. Could it be that the chemotherapy was continuing to take its toll even though it had been weeks since he had treatment, or was it that the cancer was beginning to rear its ugly head once again? I tried my best to keep strong in faith and began putting a lot of energy into preparing our home for Christmas and for all of our family who would be visiting us at that time.

December 2, 2014

Psalm 25: 4-5
"Teach me your ways oh Lord, teach me your paths; Guide me in your truth and teach me, you are God my Savior and my hope is in you all day long."

December 5, 2014

~ It's the annual Christmas party for my workplace. Loren feels well enough to be going and we are looking forward to a night out together. His blood counts are back into a normal range and he has put some weight back on. He had lost twenty pounds through the chemotherapy he underwent earlier in the fall. We dressed up and I insisted we take a photo or two before we left the house. We enjoyed ourselves while we were there, but we didn't stay long as Loren tires easily. All throughout the party so many of my co-workers commented on just "how good" Loren looked. He does, most especially in comparison to what he had looked like a few weeks earlier. However I couldn't shake the nagging feeling in my gut that something was just not right.

December 6, 2014

2 Corinthians 4:18
"So we fix our eyes not on what is seen, but on what is unseen, since what is seen is temporary, but what is unseen is eternal."

~ Oh how we have attempted to keep this in our hearts throughout this journey...It has been a good week for Loren. He has had a couple of days of "hanging with the guys". A HUGE thanks to Loren's Delta family who this week kept him part of the celebrations as the Christmas season begins in full force. Thursday his supervisor came and picked him up and brought him out to Delta where he spent several hours talking with everyone and eating pizza...eating has become a favorite pastime of his! Then, on Friday, another friend came and picked him up for the luncheon at a steak restaurant. So much enjoyment for him! It did my heart good to see what being with his Delta family did for him.

It's been a difficult week for me. I am trying so hard to hold in my heart that "HE is already there". Everywhere Loren has been this week...two visits with his Delta family and our Christmas party last night where people have the opportunity to see and speak to Loren the reaction is the same, "He looks so good!" To know where he has been in this journey, yes, he does "look good". But it is the knowing where he has been, and seeing what I see from day to day which can cause concern...and although this passage speaks to us about our Lord's faithfulness to us in our faithfulness to HIM in what we cannot see, I find the fear creeping up inside.

So, I ask that as we move closer to Christmas when we remember and celebrate the birth of our Savior to a young mother who said "yes" to THE miracle placed in her womb, that you pray for Loren and for me, that we remain strong in our belief of what is "seen and unseen" and that HE continue to keep Loren in the stable condition that we were told he was in several weeks ago.

December 7, 2014

Matthew 2: 10-11
"When they saw the star, they rejoiced with exceedingly great joy. And when they had come into the house, they saw the young Child with Mary His Mother, and fell down and worshiped Him."

~ There is so much to say, and as most of you know I can be quite "wordy". This will be our Christmas card to all of you, and a way of saying thank you to you all. Please know that we can never "say" enough nor would we be able to "do" enough to thank you for EVERYTHING you have done for us in these past eight months. The countless phone calls, private messages, cards, meals made for us by so many of you, friends who have driven Loren to appointments so that I can meet him there after

work, and those who have stayed with him during the day so I might have peace of mind and heart while trying to keep us afloat financially, and our neighbors who have taken care of our home and lawn all of these months for us. Family who cared enough to travel to Atlanta to take care of ME while Loren was hospitalized, and many who have helped us financially...some that we know, and many others who we will never know. Most of all, thank you for the endless prayers. They have kept us alive physically and spiritually. It is prayer that has given us hope in the dark of the night when there seemed to be none. It is prayer that has shielded us from the "evil one" who wanted and still wants to lead us from HIS peacefulness, and it is your prayers that we ask you to continue without ceasing as we continue this journey. Praying that all of us will find ourselves guided by the star to The Child who is The Way of Peace. God bless you all and thank you from the bottom of our hearts. ~ Libby and Loren

December 10, 2014

Isaiah 41:10
"...fear not, for I am with you; be not dismayed, for I am your God; I will strengthen you, I will help you, I will uphold you with my righteous right hand."
Jesus Calling ~
"Make ME the focal point of your search for security. In your private thoughts, you are still trying to order your world so that it is predictable and feels safe. Not only is this an impossible goal, but it is also counterproductive to spiritual growth. When your private world feels unsteady

and you grip MY hand for support, you are living in conscious dependence on ME.
Instead of yearning for a problem-free life, rejoice that trouble can highlight your awareness of MY Presence. In the darkness of adversity, you are able to see more clearly the radiance of MY Face. Accept the value of problems in this life, considering them pure joy. Remember that you have an eternity of trouble-free living awaiting you in heaven."

~ The last few days have been days of tears for me, a rarity in this eight month journey. Many things I have seen or read have caused me moments of tears. I have done my best for these past eight months to keep my emotions in check. Of course Loren's initial diagnosis and those early days, the times when the non-stop paperwork and phone calls got to me, the death of my father in June, the recurrence of Loren's cancer in July when things had seemed so promising, and how seriously ill he had become after the horrendous chemo. Twice. These are the times in the last eight months that have hit me the hardest, that have brought me to my knees, and have knocked the breath out of me. In between those moments there have been many more times that I, that we, have felt bolstered by prayers and hugs and comforting words and kind deeds. But these last few days...I'm not really sure what is happening. Is it just fatigue? After all I hit the bed by 9PM last night. When I came home today I had another rare moment...I allowed myself to spill out all the emotion to my husband. Something I have not done in the last eight months, because I did not want to burden him with my sadness, my anxieties and my fears. Today I just put it all out there, and today I was reminded of why I have always loved this man who has always allowed me to spill out my emotion to him whenever I have needed to throughout our life together. After we talked he went downstairs to read while I sat at the kitchen table once again to put our finances in check. He called up to me, "Hon, have you had a chance to read Jesus Calling today? It is talking about just what you were sharing with me." I had not...and so I did. Yes, once again, God letting me know that everything I am feeling, everything I hold in my heart...HE is already there. Thank you God, for ALWAYS letting me know YOU are there and thank you for this husband who you have allowed me to still have in my life and the moments today that helped me to remember what a gift he has been to me all these years.

Loren is continuing to regain his strength...he was ecstatic today sharing that he was able to do "a plank" for more than 20 seconds! Pretty darn good for a guy who literally had no muscle tone a month or so ago! Tomorrow we will have an appointment with the neurologist who is trying to wean Loren from one anti-seizure medication to another. He has had some side effects from doing so, so we are looking forward to meeting again with the doctor.

Asking for continued prayers and to remember that we are still walking this journey...

December 13, 2014

Ephesians 3:20
"God is able to do immeasurably more than all we ask or imagine, according to His power that is at work within us."

~ After reading Jesus Calling earlier today I have read this passage numerous times throughout this day. Having had a couple of conversations today my prayer for my family and friends is to believe this passage with all our hearts and souls..."HE is able to do IMMEASURABLY MORE THAN ALL WE ASK OR IMAGINE"...regardless of what we are experiencing in our lives.

December 14, 2014

Proverbs 3:6
"In all your ways acknowledge Him and He shall direct your paths."

~ Since coming home from Mass this morning Loren and I have sat at our kitchen table reflecting on some of the message that our pastor Father John shared with us during his homily. Beautiful and uplifting words about JOY and what that means to the Christian. What JOY brings to us and how we share it with one another. What I came away with this morning was that in order to have JOY in our lives we must have a grateful heart. As I go through my day I often hear, "I don't know how you do it", or "you always have a smile on your face". I told Loren

133

that it never really occurred to me until today that maybe the reason I am able to have the JOY that I have in my life right now, despite the journey that we are on, is because EVERY day without fail I say to our Father, "Thank you Father for one more day, another day with the gift that you brought into my life all those years ago, my husband. I may not have always recognized him as a gift in my life, but through this journey it is clearer now than it EVER has been. THANK YOU!" A grateful heart. The JOY is in the knowing, in the recognizing that each moment of each day is a gift. THAT'S how I am able to "do it". I love and am GRATEFUL for every one of you who shares your loving care and concern and your prayers for Loren and for me each day. BE JOYFUL!

December 15, 2014

~ Twenty-seven years ago today my honey and I moved our family of three little boys into this house that we built. We were so happy and excited...and so young. We knew it was going to be our "forever home", where we would raise our family. Our daughter was born two years later.....some days I would give anything to go back there to that time...

December 20, 2014

Psalm 92 1-2
""It is good to praise the Lord...to proclaim your love in the morning and your faithfulness at night."

~ Today is our daughter and son-in-law's first wedding anniversary. At times it is so hard to believe that an entire year has gone by since this wonderful day of celebration when all of our family was together and harder yet to believe what has transpired since that day. So much pain and so much happiness. But that is life, isn't it? The happy news of our son and daughter-in-law expecting another baby was followed by the news of Loren's brain cancer which was then followed by my father's death. Two days ago was the sixth month anniversary of his death...a half a year...a half a year has gone by...so hard to believe. Shortly after that Marie and Michael were deployed and that was followed by the recurrence of Loren's cancer. What had been such promising news just a few weeks earlier turned into yet another nightmare. Loren and I were talking about it the other day. We often talk about life in terms of before and after his diagnosis. He was saying that he has no idea what happened to this entire year. I do, I wish I didn't, but I do. From August to early October Loren spent more than thirty days in the hospital. I look at him now and he is like a different person than he was during that time. I look at him now and I can't even believe that he is ill....and everyone who sees him says the same thing. I look at him now and it's hard to believe that the oncologist who oversaw his care here in the hospital in our town says that he is "one resilient man and is lucky to be here". So many times in this past year I wondered and feared if we would celebrate our next anniversary. I wondered if he would be here to meet his new grandson. I wondered if his daughter and son-in-law would have to be brought back from deployment because his illness was so dire. I wondered if he would be here to celebrate his 59th birthday on the 23rd of this month or his daughter's first wedding anniversary or the Christmas season with his family. He has fought; WE have fought for ALL of these things. We have prayed and prayed and prayed without ceasing along with so many of you.

Psalm 92:1-2
"It is good to praise the Lord...to proclaim your love in the morning and your faithfulness at night."

~ We give praise to our Lord for each day and each night that we have been given and our praise continues without ceasing. That's all we can do. All we can do is continue to give praise, continue to believe that our God is an AWESOME GOD and will continue to show us that HE is THE ONE through whom ALL THINGS ARE POSSIBLE! HE has given us SO MUCH! Our family will all be together soon. We will gather strength and courage from them and on December 26th Loren will have another MRI. We will continue to have faith that God's healing hand is at work and he will continue to grow stronger and be able to return to work soon after the first of the year. God bless you all and continue to keep Loren and our family in prayer. Merry Christmas to all of you!

December 21, 2014

John 11:40
"Then Jesus said, "Did I not tell you that if you believed you would see the Glory of God?"

~ I've often heard it said, have no expectations and you won't ever be disappointed. This is most certainly the truth when it comes to relationships in our lives. I have spent too many of the 54 years of my life having "expectations" in relationships, only to be sorely disappointed. I would have to say it has only been the past half dozen years or so that I have earnestly tried to put that into practice. I'm not always successful at it, but I am trying. Today's Jesus Calling reminded me to depend on HIM for our strength to be sustained and to "expect miracles". EXPECT miracles I thought to myself. Will I only be disappointed once again if I have "EXPECTATIONS" for the miracles that HE is promising? As I sat and thought about it I realized that I have ALREADY SEEN HIS MIRACLES! I wake up and sit and stand and eat with HIS MIRACLE EVERYDAY! The miracle is my husband seen so clearly with the naked eye! He is a walking miracle! I will continue to live by faith, realizing that every single day that God has worked HIS healing hand in him, giving us one more day together is a miracle. Truthfully, one could say that each and every day ANY OF US has here is a miracle. None of us is ever promised tomorrow, but I have been able to see HIS GLORY in my life EVERY day for these past eight months.

December 22, 2014

~ Preparations for the Christmas holiday and family coming into town are in full swing. Tomorrow is my precious husband's birthday. As always he never wants much, but he asked if I would make him a lemon

137

meringue pie. Puhleeeeze! I most certainly will! Happy birthday to my precious husband!

December 23, 2014

~ Today is an incredible day of celebration. It is Loren's 59th birthday and our new grandson's baptismal day. We are so grateful that God gave us this day to share with our family.

December 24, 2014

~ It's Christmas Eve and what would an Auers' Family Christmas be without a trip to the ER? Poor Loren. He had a weak spell this morning while trying to treat his family to a pancake breakfast. We're not sure exactly how or why it happened, but let's just say the George Foreman grill - 1, Loren - 0. Loren has badly burned his hand. We are sitting in Grady's trauma center. Our son who is an EMT thought it should be looked at. When asked by the nurse what they could do to help today Loren replied, "You can get me outta here in a hurry." Love him.

December 25, 2014

~ Loren spent a comfortable night at home and the morning is filled with our grandchildren's excitement over Santa's visit. We are doing our best to enjoy the moments throughout the day with very little talk of the MRI to come tomorrow.

December 26, 2014

~ Loren had his MRI today. We do our best to wait for the phone call from his neuro-oncologist patiently and without anxiety. The phone call did not come today.

December 27, 2014

Psalm 36:9
"For with You is the fountain of life; in Your light do we see light."

Jesus Calling ~
"I am preparing you for what is on the road ahead, just around the bend. Take time to be still in My Presence so that I can strengthen you. The busier you become, the more you need this time apart with Me. So many people think that time spent with Me is a luxury they cannot afford. As a result, they live and work in their own strength—until that becomes depleted. Then they either cry out to Me for help or turn away in bitterness."

~ Loren had an MRI yesterday. This morning at 8:30 Dr. Dunbar called with the results. One lesion has remained stable, the other has grown. According to her it is "not an emergency situation", but enough growth and apparently swelling for her to want to put him on steroids. She will consult with her colleagues around the country early next week as to what direction to move for further treatment. I have noticed some changes in Loren in the past several weeks which have concerned me, so I have to say that I was not surprised to hear this news, but at the same time I was still disheartened. Loren will probably be returning to the hospital for treatment the week after next. News to us this morning from Dr. Dunbar is that Loren has a "rare grade" of this particular type of lymphoma which is why it is making it so hard to fight. But he will continue to fight...until God shows us HIS will for us. For HE is the "fountain of life" and in HIM we place our trust. After our phone call with Dr. Dunbar I read todays Jesus Calling. The "road ahead" I'm not sure of, but I do know that we will continue to trust...Please continue to pray without ceasing for my husband.

December 28, 2014

~ We are doing our best to stay positive while waiting on word from Dr. Dunbar as to how to continue the fight with Loren's cancer. While we wait I realize that our life is forever marked by the before and the after of Loren's diagnosis and we will never be the same...

December 29, 2014

~ Today we had an unexpected visit from our little grandsons. They bring such joy to our lives...and their Papa brings such joy to them. A little trip out for a bite to eat for dinner was enjoyed as well.

Jesus Calling ~
"Trust Me with every fiber of your being! What I can accomplish in and through you is proportional to how much you depend on Me. One aspect of this is the degree to which you trust Me in a crisis or major decision. Some people fail miserably here, while others are at their best

in tough times. Another aspect is even more telling: the constancy of your trust in Me. People who rely on Me in the midst of adversity may forget about Me when life is flowing smoothly. Difficult times can jolt you into awareness of your need for Me, whereas smooth sailing can lull you into the stupor of self-sufficiency.

I care as much about your tiny trust-steps through daily life as about your dramatic leaps of faith. You may think that no one notices, but the One who is always beside you sees everything—and rejoices. Consistently trusting in Me is vital to flourishing in My Presence."

December 31, 2014

1 Thessalonians 5: 16-18
"What if your blessings come through raindrops? What if your healing comes through tears? What if a thousand sleepless nights are what it takes to know your near? What if trials of this life are your mercies in disguise?"

~ The end of a year with so many trials and so many tears...what will the new year bring? Help me Dear Father to know YOU are always by our side.

JANUARY 2015

January 3, 2015

John 16:33
"I have told you these things, so that in Me you may have peace. In this world you will have trouble, but take heart! I have overcome the world."

January 4, 2015

~ I've been spending time looking through photos today...as I look at these photos that melt my heart of Loren and our little grandson back in 2013 my heart skips a beat as I wonder, will he get to do these things with our new little grandson born in October? I have thought about how in 2013 there was not even an inkling of what we would face in 2014 and about how what we have experienced in this past year is a reason to cherish every moment of every day. None of us is promised tomorrow. Today our pastor Father John spoke about how God has a path for each of us to follow. Loren and I have spoken about that many times in the past eight months, most especially when we talk about our past and what our future may hold. We talk about how hard it is to "plan things". We don't understand it, and we definitely don't want this plan...this journey. The last week has been a difficult one as the results of Loren's MRI leaves us wondering, "what now?" And, "where does this journey go from here?" Of course only God knows the answer to these questions. So our prayer to HIM is to strengthen us and give us peace. God bless.

January 5, 2015

Psalm 56: 8
"Tears are prayers too. They travel to God when we can't
speak."

January 6, 2015

Ephesians 3: 20
"Now to Him who is able to do immeasurably more than
all we ask or imagine according to His power that is at
work within us."

~ There is one thing I know for sure about my husband after all these years. It is that his faith runs deeper than most any person I know, a quiet deep faith. I also know that my faith will NEVER be as strong or unwavering as his is.

A couple of days ago Loren had a conversation with me about an article that he read. It was about a seventeen year old girl who has cancer and apparently she wants to refuse chemotherapy. I'm not quite clear about all the facts. Today when I came home from work we were sitting together at the kitchen table. It seems we have our best conversations sitting here for some reason. Some conversations I would rather not have, others are enjoyable and light hearted. Those are the ones I'd rather have, but as you might imagine, given our present circumstances there are times that we must face the reality of our situation. When Loren read this article about the seventeen year old it must have prompted thoughts about his own treatment and what he wants to do. Although he didn't come right out and say it in so many words he must have given a good bit of thought to when or if he would put a stop to his own treatment. He didn't discuss that with me until today. Alone here in the house while reading Jesus Calling he said, "The Spirit spoke to me and I realized that I am not ready to end my treatments. God is not done with me yet." It brought up so many emotions in me. One was fear. Fear that he must have been at a point where he may have contemplated stopping his treatments. Another was gratitude. Gratitude that my husband's faith is so deep that he clearly heard and felt The Spirit and that The Spirit shared with him that there is more planned for him. So, as difficult as these last couple of weeks have been for me, physically, emotionally and most definitely spiritually, I will fight on with and for Loren, because The Spirit has instilled in him that this is what we must do. Please continue to pray for our strength and for God to show HIS MIGHTY POWER for complete healing for Loren.

January 9, 2015

~ This afternoon I was blessed by a couple of people who stood next to me and listened...after my answer to their question "How are you?" was "I'm fine." Thank you for blessing me with ears to listen and a hug...a real hug, as I stood there with tears in my eyes. I truly, truly appreciate you. Today Loren had blood work done and an appointment with the oncologist that took over his care while he was hospitalized in September and October here in our local hospital. He was very happy to see the results of Loren's blood work. In fact he said, "Your blood work looks spectacular!" It surely seems odd to hear that with what we know about Loren's health, but we praise God that His healing hand has been at work in Loren. HE has been preparing Loren's body for his next bout of chemo, whenever that may be. One thing Loren's neuro-oncologist wants to do is begin treatment with one of the medications that had been used as part of his chemo treatments. Technically it is not chemo, but it is used as part of the treatment against lymphoma. The doctor we saw today was discussing that with us, and the fact that it can be done as an outpatient in his facility. That is wonderful news that Loren won't have to be hospitalized while this medication is administered.

In recent weeks you could say that I've had an epiphany of sorts. Although many people have used this word over and over in their conversations with me, "CAREGIVER", I suppose I never really saw myself in that roll. Since last April I've just gone day by day, doing what I've been doing, day in and day out. I've never really thought of myself as the "caregiver". However recently, maybe it's fatigue that is catching up with me; I "feel" every bit the caregiver. And so, I am going to do what a good caregiver does, and what has been suggested many times over in the last nine months to me, and something that I haven't been that good about. I am going to reach out to all of you. We have been so fortunate to have friends, who when Loren was not well and pretty weak, would come to stay with him throughout the day. Now that he is stronger we haven't had them coming. It would be nice for people to call in and check up on him...he won't admit it, but I think he is lonely. This is not a good place for him to be in. It isn't for anyone. I at least have people around me in the workplace. He doesn't have that. He was hopeful that he would be preparing to head back to work. It doesn't look like that is happening any time soon now with the recurrence. When you are dealing with a serious illness it is important to know that there are people praying for you. But it is also important for that person and their caregiver to be sent cards, notes, text messages, emails, and Facebook messages. They may not always be answered, but these things will let Loren know that he has not been forgotten. Phone calls may or may not be answered, you see sometimes by the end of a day you have no energy left, so to be expending energy on the phone rehashing what is happening with Loren's health or treatment is just way too much, but to be able to physically read a message and be able to know that you are thought of can be energizing....and truly life giving. So, I want to say thank you to you all for your continued prayers and ask that you reach out to Loren as his doctor would say, "as we begin this next chapter" in Loren's care.

January 11, 2015

Colossians 4: 2
"Devote yourselves to prayer, being watchful and thankful."

~ Today's devotion in Jesus Calling talks about relinquishing control. "Relinquishing control"...Ah, something Libby has never been very good at, even with

God. That is one tall order being asked of me, but as I continued to read todays Jesus Calling I realized that perhaps this is why I cannot have the "peace" I pray for every day. I have laid out my concerns, my sorrows, and my fears to HIM every day, and yet my heart seems in turmoil, every moment of every day. Ah! God knows my concerns already! In fact, HE's probably tired of me repeating them to HIM over and over again. I've lost my "thankfulness" recently. Thankful that Loren's body continues to get stronger. Thankful that we wake up to another day together. Thankful that I have remained healthy through this journey. Thankful for HIS hand putting me in a place each day that I find joy and can bring that home to share with Loren each day. Thankful for so many things....but through my weariness I've been forgetting to say that to HIM. I've got to leave the litany of burdens and fears out and make it a litany of THANKS, realizing that I have spoken to HIM about them already. HE hasn't forgotten. HE has already set into motion HIS answer, and regardless of what the answer may be I need to remain thankful to HIM. I see it; I just have to learn to surrender to it....hard to change old habits.

January 12, 2015

Exodus 33: 14
"My Presence will go with you, and I will give you rest."

January 13, 2015

1 Peter 2: 21
"For to this you were called; because Christ also suffered for us, leaving us an example, that you should follow His steps..."

*****

Romans 15: 13
"May the God of hope fill you with all Joy and Peace as you Trust in Him."

~ It's been more than two hours waiting for Loren while he's having his MRI...just received a message from the neuro oncologist's office. The radiologist here requested his previous scans for comparison twenty minutes ago. Dear Lord in Heaven, give me strength...and courage.

January 14, 2015

~ The first thing I would like to share is that I called the doctor's office this morning to see if they had received the report from Loren's MRI. They had, and the report was good news. Nothing was showing in the MRI that would cause them to believe that the lymphoma was in Loren's spine at all. Tomorrow Loren will have the first of several outpatient infusions. This afternoon he expressed anxiety over having the treatment even though it is one of the medications used to treat him during previous chemo treatments. I'm not sure why he feels like that. I'm not sure if it is the steroids he has been on since we first found out about the recurrence as they can affect your mood. Please pray for a peaceful heart for Loren and that the treatment halts the growth of the cancer until Dr. Dunbar can decide what direction to take next.

Today after my phone call to the doctor I spent time talking with one of my beautiful friends at work...talking may not be the appropriate word. The flood gates opened, and Dear Lord, how good it felt afterward. God most certainly showed HIS love for me today with the people HE has placed in my life. I want to share my thanks and gratefulness to HIM who allowed me this time with my friend today...and to my incredible co-worker who never tires of listening to me, (or at least she doesn't seem to) when I need someone to listen. Thank you Father for loving me with the people YOU have put in my life!

January 16, 2015

Joshua 1: 9
"Be strong and courageous, have no fear and do not be troubled for the Lord your God will be with you wherever you go."

~ ...This has been the hardest of all things that God has asked of me, of us, during this journey. Day in and day out it is a struggle, but HE knows what is in my heart. HE knows my fears, my anxieties, and my struggles and HE continues to hold my hand through it all. HE is already there...and will be with me wherever I go....

January 17, 2015

Philippians 4: 6-7
*"Be anxious for nothing, but in everything by prayer and
supplication, with thanksgiving, let your requests be
known to God, which surpasses all understanding, will
guard your hearts and minds through Christ Jesus.*

~ Oh my yes...I freely admit that I have been having
difficulty praying lately, but I still do it. I also have been
trying to remember, as I said recently, that God fully
knows what our needs are since I have prayed of them
often, and I am trying to leave the requesting behind and
be more thankful. Yesterday I was reminded of how
much God knows our needs and the ways that HE goes
about showing us that HE is in control and "loves us
through HIS people". Loren texted me at work yesterday
and told me that his supervisor was coming by to visit
and had something for him. When I came home from
work there was a card sitting on the kitchen table. In it
was an incredible gift to us from his many co-workers.
God is good! My heart has been heavy with the burden of
a new year and new medical costs that will begin to add
up and I have wanted to take care of another financial
burden for some time now. I've been working on it, slow
and steady, but still it has been weighing on my mind.
Last night we went out to run some errands and put gas
in the car. As we were pulling into the grocery store
Loren said, "I think I'll buy a lottery ticket, it's up there!"
Old habits die hard! For as many years as I can
remember, on his way home from work on Fridays,
Loren would buy a lottery ticket. I think the most he ever

won was $88 dollars. Crack me up. But, our children all went to college on the Hope Scholarship from the state of Georgia, so I guess it wasn't all so bad. I responded to him by asking, "Why do you feel the need to do that? God is giving us everything we need right now. Did HE not just show you that this afternoon?" He said, "You know, you are right." Last night I received a phone call from a friend who was talking to me about possibly another way I could earn a little extra money. I'm not quite sure how it will work out, but I went to bed last night hopeful AND thankful to our God who opened my eyes to HIS wondrous hand at work in our lives. Sometimes I need more than subtlety! So, with a heart full of gratitude I want to acknowledge our Delta family for their amazing generosity, care and concern for Loren and for me. We are so thankful to you all! Please continue to pray for Loren as he continues his treatments and that God will help Dr. Dunbar and her colleagues find the answers they are looking for to treat Loren and bring him to complete healing. God Bless.

January 18, 2015

2 Timothy 4: 17
"But the Lord stood at my side and gave me strength."

January 20, 2015

Psalm 16: 8
"I will keep my eyes always on the Lord. With Him at my right hand, I will not be shaken."

~ After several days of seeing numerous symptoms returning with Loren we decided it would be prudent to go to the ER for Loren to be looked at. I had contacted Dr. Dunbar's office prior to us going. Once at the hospital they took Loren for an MRI, and our instincts were correct. There has been growth once again in the cancer. Significant inflammation has occurred and they began heavier steroid treatment to bring the inflammation down. One of the ventricles, much like when Loren was first diagnosed, is showing fluid buildup. They are not sure at this time if there is something actually blocking the ventricle or if it is the inflammation causing it.

They have admitted Loren to the hospital and Dr. Dunbar will see us in the morning. She was able to come to the ER and share a few things with us before she had to be at a meeting. One thing she shared is that Loren's treatment he had last week has not had the opportunity to work yet. That being said, she did mention possibly beginning some form of chemo treatment. That's all we know at this point.

Before we left for the hospital this morning Loren shared some very emotional moments with me. But most of all he spoke again, as he does so often, of his faith in our Lord and that he accepts HIS will as we walk this road with HIM.

We ask that you continue your prayers for healing, strength and peace and we want you to know how much we love you all. God Bless.

*****

Psalm 56: 3-4
"When I am afraid I put my trust in You, in God whose
word I praise, in God I trust and I am not afraid. What
can mere mortals do to me?"

✻✻✻✻✻

~ I am sitting here with Loren and reading him all of your words of support and prayers for him. He has asked me to tell you how much he appreciates all of you and "thank you so much".

January 21, 2015

~ I had a "God Moment" this evening....some of you may know this story. April 19th, 2014. I remember the details of that day so clearly, as if it happened only yesterday...even though I can barely remember yesterday. After Loren was diagnosed in our local hospital he was transported up to Atlanta. He was placed in a room on the 4th floor of the hospital. They monitored him for several hours. We had the most wonderful nurse. He was caring, compassionate and kind. We only saw a doctor for a few minutes that night as Loren was clearly a brain cancer patient and Dr. Dunbar, whose care Loren had already been placed under, was returning the next day from Florida.

About 12:30 in the morning our nurse came to the foot of the pull out bed I was on and said, "They are moving your husband to ICU." I was confused as to why they would do that. I thought things were under control; after all, no doctor had spent any amount of time with us since we had arrived. I asked, "When?" And he said

"Now." I was frightened and by myself, but I gathered up all our things and we trudged off down the hallway.

There are no bathrooms in ICU so several times during the night I would have to walk out of ICU and back down the hallway to use the bathrooms in the waiting area. About 4AM after a number of times through the hallways our nurse stopped me and asked me several questions. "Are you doing okay? Are you all by yourself? Is anyone coming to be with you?" And "Has anyone come and told you anything about your husband?" To which I answered "No"...he took me down the hallway and shared what he knew about Loren's situation. I was shocked by the gravity of what he shared, but so relieved that I finally had an answer as to why he had been moved to ICU. Most of all, I was so touched by this young man and his concern for me.

Loren spent several days in ICU before they moved him to the 2nd floor to begin his first chemo treatment. We spent weeks going to chemo from April through the end of June and several times I made a trip up to the 4th floor to see if I could find this young man who had made such an impact on me in those first hours after finding out that my husband had brain cancer. I never saw him again...until tonight!

Earlier I realized I didn't have my reflux medication and I could tell already that I was going to need it. There is a drugstore right across the street from the hospital....I could see it from the window of our room. It's opened all night. But I didn't want to walk across the street by myself...hey, it's Atlanta and it was late at night. Our lovely nurse said she would be happy to get someone to walk with me. Off she went, and in she walked saying, "I found you your guardian angel." Low and behold it was him! "Guardian angel" indeed! I was so thrilled to see him and so happy that I had the opportunity to share with him how much he meant to me in those hours after Loren's diagnosis. He was so touched that I remembered him and that what he did that night would mean so much to me. I told him how I had searched for him many times. He told me that he had left there in May and had just recently come back because he missed being there so much. I hope my conversation with him blessed him as much as he blessed me that night in April. I told him that I wholeheartedly believe that God sends us HIS angels when HE knows we need them the most...like that night in April...like tonight, when all of those same fears and anxieties are there. I am so thankful that God gave me the opportunity to finally be able to thank this incredibly kind and compassionate "angel".

*****

~ First, we would like to thank all of you for your continued prayers of healing, strength, courage and peace for us as this journey continues. We love you all from the bottom of our hearts.

We are home. Loren was discharged this afternoon. His condition was stable enough that Dr. Dunbar felt confident to let him come home so that we can continue with his treatments tomorrow closer to home.

Dr. Dunbar came to see us this morning and brought with her a radiologist who serves both Atlanta and Fayetteville. Dr. Dunbar drew a diagram for us of what is happening with the lymphoma. The one tumor that they have been keeping a close eye on has grown significantly. What they feel is happening, and they cannot know this with one hundred percent accuracy because they cannot actually get to it to see it, is that they believe that there are microscopic cells which are lining the ventricle wall and that are causing the blockage and fluid buildup. The best way right now to treat that type of scenario is full brain radiation. If Dr. Dunbar was to use chemotherapy for this situation she would have to use extremely strong medicines which would probably put Loren into the dangerous situation he was in a couple of months ago and she is trying to avoid that the best she can. The radiologist spent a good bit of time with us explaining the process and the expectations of the radiation treatment. He seems like a really terrific doctor. So we will meet with him after Loren's treatment tomorrow and he will map out a plan. What we do know is that there will be ten treatments, most likely beginning on Monday. Dr. Dunbar wants to meet with us in a couple of weeks. In all probability we will discuss further chemo at that time and what type. She says it is possible it could be oral medication.

One day, one moment at a time...

Again, thank you all. Prayers of wisdom for the doctors and complete healing and peace of mind and heart are what's needed. God Bless.

January 22, 2015

"Believers, look up, take courage, the angels are nearer than you think." ~ Billy Graham

~ It has been several days of God reminding me moment by moment how HE is here. HE is walking beside us by "loving us through HIS people", HIS angels on earth. If you stop and take a breath and open your heart to it, you see them...daily. Today I was reminded once again how HE has blessed me by putting me back in my "home"...my "refuge" as my boss said to me today. He is so right. I have looked at my "home" on The Hill as my refuge. They are the angels that I have in my life, every day. Those that let me cry, that listen with an open heart. Two in particular who have such wisdom and are true women of faith. They allow me to be angry and sorrowful without judging me but offer unconditional love and comfort to me. God's angels in my life and I am thankful EVERY single day that HE has gifted my life with them.

I also spent time talking with the man who has been my boss for several years now. His compassion and concern for what we are going through gave me a measure of peace that I haven't felt for a while now and I am so very thankful for the time spent speaking with him today. Many God Moments for me in the past few days.

I also am so grateful for all of our friends...our Angel Caregivers who have been here for us relieving our anxiety and stress when we are feeling overwhelmed by our journey. We so love all of you.

Today Loren had his second infusion treatment. It went really well. No reactions and they were able to speed up the process enabling us to get to the appointment with the radiologist who will be doing Loren's radiation treatments. While we were taken aback by some misinformation we received yesterday from him, we also were given a renewed hope today. He asked us to forgive him in that he had a "momentary brain fart"...his words, not mine! Loren will be receiving twenty-three radiation treatments, not ten as we were first told in the hospital. He shared with us that that is actually good news. Ten treatments would actually have been used as a palliative intent and not a CURATIVE intent. We haven't heard that word in a positive way for a while now. So, we left the radiologist's office with a much better outlook on Loren's treatment. PRAISE GOD!

I told Loren when we were coming home, that this morning while I was getting ready I had a clear vision of Jesus's resurrection. In that moment I told God that HE and HIS SON had shown us the ultimate miracle...HIS SON being given NEW LIFE...HE WAS DEAD AND NOW HE IS ALIVE. I told HIM I know HE can do the same for Loren; I know HE can perform this miracle of healing in Loren. HE CAN...and then we received the news from the radiologist..."curative intent". Oh Dear God in Heaven! YES! YOU CAN!

January 25, 2015

~ Good morning family, friends and angel caregivers, this Sunday morning finds us at home rather than at Mass, as Loren is still quite weak with other symptoms from this latest recurrence. I was told on Thursday that we would be seeing improvement in those symptoms by the end of the weekend because of the steroids he is taking, but that hasn't happened. The fear wants to take over, but I am more hopeful that tomorrow as he begins his radiation treatments that he will begin to improve.

*****

~ We were able to watch a video today online of someone we have met through our journey. The video also features Dr. Erin Dunbar who has been walking this journey with us since April 19, 2014. She is beautiful inside and out. She is brilliant and a woman of deep faith. She knows that EVERYTHING she does, and everything she has to offer her patients comes from a greater power. She always ends a phone call with, "know that you are in my thoughts and prayers." She never forgets that these are, as she says often, "tender moments" for her patients and their families. We have been blessed to have her in our life.

January 26, 2015

~ I have laid here awake since 4AM and so many thoughts are going through my head. Will Loren be doing better today? He's had a good night. I found myself reaching over a couple of times to put my hand on his back to check his breathing as he has been so still throughout the night. But mostly I have laid here thinking about our daughter-in-law. She has always impressed me with her quiet strength. When she first came into our lives she was a very timid person but it was clear she was strong and so very intelligent. Throughout the years we have come to know that all of those things are true. She has always loved and respected us. This morning while I've thought of her, I have thought

160

how very thankful I am that she is in our lives. She is a physical therapy assistant. A perfect profession for her, with her physical strength but more importantly her ability to show how much she cares for the patients she works with. I know this because yesterday my husband, her father-in-law, was her patient. She was loving and caring and showed us her strength and she showed me how to best help Loren. While she worked with us she never made Loren feel that he was not capable, in fact, she encouraged him with her gentle words and quiet demeanor while assisting the two of us. She stayed the night and assured us that she would be here in a heartbeat if I needed her. Through her guidance I found the strength and the courage to know that I could do what I needed to do to help Loren. We are and have been so blessed to have her in our lives. She has brought so much joy to our lives by giving us our two precious grandbabies and we love her dearly.

*****

~ Today Loren will have his first of twenty-three radiation treatments. I ask that you keep him in prayer. The doctors are looking at this in a very positive light and so we are trusting in their God given abilities. We trust that God has given them the wisdom to know that this is the right direction to go in for the miracle of God's healing hand. Let us follow HIM more nearly as he leads us on this journey. God Bless.

January 27, 2015

John 14:27
"Peace I leave with you, my peace I give to you; not as the
world gives do I give to you. Let not your heart be
troubled, neither let it be afraid."

*****

It has been a very difficult week. Last Tuesday we were in the ER in Atlanta. Loren had an MRI where it was found that the recurrence they diagnosed the day after Christmas had gotten larger and was affecting the ventricle on the left side of his brain. They admitted him and gave him large doses of IV steroids to bring the inflammation down. They discharged him on Wednesday afternoon and increased his oral steroids telling us that his condition should improve in the next couple of days. It hasn't, in fact his condition has become much worse.

~ DAMN THIS BRAIN CANCER!!!

His cognitive abilities are a bit jumbled and his physical abilities are becoming extremely limited. Even a simple task like taking his medications is very difficult. He has trouble picking up his medications and his hand to mouth coordination is not very good. You know, there's that saying that so many people have quoted to me in the past nine months. "You never know how strong you are until being strong is the only choice you have." I have never known the full meaning of this quote until this very point in time. I've always put myself down for how "out of shape" I am. Today I realized just how strong I am. Loren had his second radiation treatment today.

Let's just say that getting him in and out of the car right now is no easy task. When he was taken back to have his radiation I informed them that they were going to have to give him quite a bit of assistance to get him on the table. "Oh no problem, we have Mr. Larry and he can get him on up there." Well, hooray for "Mr. Larry". A few minutes later they came out to get the harness belt that my daughter-in-law taught me how to use to assist Loren. Loren told me when I was taking him out to the car that the tech who was working with him asked, "Your wife is able to get you in and out of the car by herself?" He said, "Yeah, she's one tough lady!" I Love him.

He doesn't know that every time I go to help him I pray to the Holy Spirit asking the Spirit to give me strength...of mind and body. My daughter-in-law taught me the mechanics and so far I have been able to keep Loren safe. I don't always have the patience...she didn't teach me that...

We saw the radiologist prior to Loren's treatment. They have increased his steroids once again. Please pray that this is what Loren's body needs to bring the inflammation down so that Loren is able to get around once again on his own. "Quality of life". We have heard that phrase time and again through this journey and right now that is all I want for him. I am sure it can't be easy for him to have me helping him in the ways I am having to. I have had to remind him many times recently that THIS was what it meant all those years ago when we took our vows..."for better or for worse, in sickness and in health"...THIS is what that meant. As always he remains hopeful and prayerful. His faith is extraordinary.

163

*****

~ I love my daughter and her precious husband. She called this afternoon to say she was on her way home from Oklahoma. She knows how difficult things have been for us lately. Although I protested she said, "I'm going to talk to Michael"...next thing I knew she is at the airport in Oklahoma City heading to Atlanta. Thank you Michael for loving Mimi the way you do and supporting her through this very difficult time.

January 28, 2015

~ The last few days of our lives have been full of things that I would never have thought we would be dealing with, at least as far as Loren is concerned. In our thirty-four years of marriage I have always teased Loren that he would be taking care of me in the future. Never did I think that at 59 years old and being in the kind of condition he had kept himself in through all these years would I think our days would consist of wheelchairs, tub chairs, harnesses to help with stability, and as has been the case since his first hospitalization, a small pharmacy of prescriptions. Which, by the way, change nearly every week. I sit and think about it and if I allow myself to stay there it would most certainly overcome me. Although we are living this life, it so often seems surreal to me. "Do not boast about tomorrow for you do not know what a day may bring"... Dear God how true. So many times throughout this journey I've had many people say how much my journaling has meant to them, how much it affects them. I truly hope that today's post does. These experiences are a harsh reality in my life and tomorrow they may be in yours. "We are never promised tomorrow"...how very true. Tomorrow may change your life forever. Ours has been.

Today Loren had his third radiation treatment. So far they have gone well for him and this evening he seems to be improving since the increase in steroids yesterday. He seems a bit more stable in his motion. Praise God! Praying tomorrow will be even better! He will have his third infusion treatment and then his fourth radiation treatment afterward.

Continued prayers....cherish today, tomorrow, and every day afterward for we know not what the day may bring.

Huge hugs to our daughter Marie who has been an amazing support through the day today. Putting together tub chairs AND a bit of plumbing as she put up a shower sprayer so Loren could more easily get cleaned up. We so love her!

January 29, 2015

Isaiah 26: 3
"You keep him in perfect peace whose mind is stayed on You, because he trusts in You."

~ It has been a long day...up early this morning and out the door for Loren's blood work and infusion. Blood counts are dropping off...one doctor's office seems concerned, the other not so much. Trusting in the Lord...Loren's physical strength continues to improve. The radiologist was encouraged that with the increase of steroids the edema symptoms will continue to improve. He says there is always the possibility that the symptoms could be caused by the tumor causing damage, in which case there would not be improvement in the symptoms. He felt confident after spending time with Loren this afternoon that that was not the case. We are thankful to God for his infinite mercies. With the drop in Loren's white cell count we now have to add in daily shots to help get his white count up. We are exhausted from the seemingly endless doctor appointments. The radiologist also wants Loren to begin some physical therapy. Pray without ceasing!

January 30, 2015

Psalm 112: 7
"They will have no fear of bad news; their hearts are steadfast, trusting in the Lord."

~ ...as always Loren is steadfast and trusting in the Lord.

Five days of radiation down...and as we were told would happen, Loren is feeling the fatigue. He hasn't completely been able to come back from the inflammation due to the growth of the tumor which is causing fatigue in itself. He has made a lot of progress in the last day and we are so thankful to our God. We will "not fear bad news"...in fact, we hold steadfast in our belief that God will work a miracle in Loren through the doctors and the tools HE has given them.

We are praying that next week will be "back to normal"... our "new normal". We shall see. Loren still needs assistance with moving from place to place, for safeties sake, and with his white count low we pretty much need to stay close to home. This is difficult in itself with the many doctor appointments we have in the next several weeks.

Next week we will meet with Loren's neuro-oncologist Dr. Dunbar, as well as continue radiation treatments and infusions, and now daily shots for the white blood cell count. Asking for continued prayers for Loren for complete healing and that he stay healthy on his journey to that healing. God Bless.

January 31, 2015

~ We just said goodbye to our daughter. She has been a huge help these last few days...physically and emotionally. I miss her already.

FEBRUARY 2015

February 2, 2015

Psalm 105: 4
"Look to the Lord and his strength; seek His face always."

~ I have never sought the Lord's strength or HIS face more than I have in the past nine months. Most certainly in the most recent couple of weeks. I am more assured than I have ever been in my life that HE walks beside me and Loren each and every day, helping us through every trial and tribulation. It gives us a certain peace as this journey continues.

Today I returned to work a half day. It was difficult leaving Loren but I am trying to balance our life the best I can. I am so grateful to our God who put me in a place where I am told unconditionally that my place is with Loren and that I will be supported in any way that I need and that this workplace is indeed my "refuge". Thank you my Spring Hill family.

Loren had more blood work today and an injection for his white cell count. His white cell count was back into a "normal" range and I am hopeful that with the injection it will climb up more. Afterward he went for his radiation treatment. The radiologist was extremely pleased when he saw Loren afterward. Loren's condition is MUCH improved since last week. That being said, he is still a bit unstable and he struggles with his short term memory, but both of those are improved since last week...AND he was able to get around without the assistance of a wheelchair! Like I said, his doctor was very, very happy with that. PRAISING GOD who continues to show us that HE is THE ONE who has the ability to heal... HE has and we believe HE will continue to! And we will continue to "Look to the Lord and HIS strength, seeking HIS face ALWAYS!"

February 4, 2015

Psalm 13: 5-6
"But I trust in your unfailing love; my heart rejoices in your salvation. I will sing the Lord's praise, for He has been good to me."

~ Loren continues to find strength in his faith and as he shared with me the other night, "I wouldn't necessarily want cancer, but through this journey I have strengthened my relationship with God and I am so thankful for that." How I love this man who continues to find the good in this horrific journey. Last night we decided we needed a Big Mac! So off we went. While we were sitting there eating Loren looked at me and said, "I'm really happy right now. I feel pretty good...I'm just happy." I wanted to cry...but I didn't. I wanted to feel that happiness with him in that moment, even if I wasn't exactly in a "happy" place. He amazes me each and every day.

Today we went to Atlanta to see Dr. Dunbar, Loren's neuro-oncologist. It was a good visit with great quality time. She is pleased with what she sees. She asked us where we wanted to go with treatment. I'm not sure what she was getting at, but it opened the door to a conversation I had with Loren the morning we left for the

170

ER in Atlanta a couple of weeks ago with his recurrence. He told me that morning that sometimes he wishes he had never started treatment. Dr. Dunbar said that "it was not lost on her how difficult a journey this has been and what a tender subject this is". She told us that she was so proud of the grace and dignity that both of us have had on this journey, but that at any time if it were Loren's decision, she would seek the best way for Loren to be taken care of if he were to decide to let the lymphoma "take a natural progression"...Each day we pray that God will work a miracle in Loren so that that decision will not EVER have to be made. Our "trust in His unfailing love" is endless.

We are thankful to all of you who have walked this journey with us by prayer, love and support in so many ways. God bless you all!

February 10, 2015

~ "God never gives you more than you can handle"... Throughout these nine months I have heard this more times than I can count. Often it is hard for me to keep my eyes from rolling back into my head. In the past month these words resonate in my head for so many reasons. I have told several people when they have said it, "then I'm ready to call 'uncle' " and frankly, I wish God didn't trust us so much. Yesterday I had an incredible conversation with one of my co-workers. He said these words and then said, "I know you've heard these words a million times." "Yes," I responded, and then I told him "I'm ready to call 'uncle'". He said to me, "Libby, maybe that is EXACTLY what HE wants you to do"....hmmm, food for thought

today for the "control freak". Now, how do I figure out
how to relinquish control...even to God...?

February 11, 2015

Hebrews 12:3
"Consider Him who endured such opposition from sinner,
so that you will not grow weary and lose heart."

February 14, 2015

Corinthians 13: 4-13
"Love is patient. Love is kind…"

~ Most of us have read these beautiful words from
Corinthians and I'm quite certain like me, you have read
them many times. Maybe, like me, you have asked
yourself "Am I?" When it comes to our spouse or
significant other, our families, are we all of these things?
In all honesty I have to admit throughout my life I have
not been. Certainly I have found these things to be
difficult throughout this road Loren and I have been on.
The overwhelming fatigue and concerns of the day set in
and I find myself at times not being kind, not being
patient...not always being hopeful. I feel envious of those
I love when I see that they are living life to the fullest.

I fixed my sweetheart some French toast this
morning...his request. While I was cleaning up breakfast
he sat talking with me. He has been reading a book that
one of my friends gave to us, "Trustful Surrender To
Divine Providence. The Secret of Peace and Happiness".
Yet another conversation with Loren where he shared

that he has given himself over to God's will. That he had a conversation with God "thanking him for his cancer". I turned and looked at him and told him that I had been thinking a lot about that since the last time he had shared that with me. I told him I was not there yet. I didn't know if I would ever be "there". I am thankful for many, many things during this journey. I am thankful that God has continued to give us this time together. I am thankful that HE has shown us HIS love through HIS people, and that I have been able to accept that love with a gracious heart. All of you, family, friends, co-workers (his and mine) that have been here loving and caring for us in so many ways. Those of you who have been here with Loren during the day, those who have helped us financially, those of you who have brought us food, and have helped to take care of our lawn for us...and most importantly prayers, prayers and more prayers. These are the things I am thankful for...but not the cancer. I told Loren sometimes I can be doing something in the house and a memory will pop into my head. Simple, sweet memories like when all the kids were growing up... I'm in the kitchen fixing dinner and Loren has been outside mowing the lawn or fixing the car or any of the many things he would do...then I would call the kids and him in for dinner and we would gather around the table to eat. A time when there didn't seem to be a care in the world...but for the everyday inconveniences of life. The things that we gripe and complain about when the reality is they shouldn't really mean a thing. What I wouldn't do to just have those "little inconveniences of life" be the only things to have to be concerned about. How often I hear these kinds of things...in the workplace, standing in line at the grocery store or post office...realizing that "everyone has a story"...some of us have a few more chapters to ours than others. I often find myself wanting to tap them on the shoulder and say, "please say a prayer of thanksgiving right now, these are the little things in life". I know I have always been a type A personality...always in a hurry, always wanting things done to perfection (if there is such a thing) and so much more. Rushing through life, not taking the time to enjoy and "cherish the moment". So many of those moments I want back. Today being Valentine's Day, take the time to cherish the moments with your loved ones. Commit to being patient, to being kind and making those loving moments endure....love and life are so very precious. Happy Valentine's Day.

February 17, 2015

2 Corinthians 5:17
"Therefore if anyone is in Christ, he is a new creature; the old things passed away; behold, new things have come."

~ How many times I have thought about my relationship in and with Christ these past nine months and how many of my old ways have passed away and the new have come? I do struggle daily with the "old ways" but give praise each day to God who strengthens me and has me believing in HIM more deeply than I have ever in my life. How could I not? I watch my husband living at peace with all that he is experiencing because he has put his trust fully in God. Yesterday I walked into the room as he sat in his chair. He had his eyes closed. I was alarmed at first and I asked him if he was alright. He looked up and said, "Yes, I was just meditating. I close my eyes often throughout the day and pray." Always, he is always in prayer. I want to be like him. I want, no matter how exhausted I am, to offer up prayer continually to our God. I will keep working on that.

Last night I went to bed exhausted. It seems to be a permanent state. I was also extremely nauseated, which also seems to be a permanent state anymore when I lay down to sleep at night. I laid there and attempted to pray. To be thankful for ALL things in my life, like my husband has been. My mind would not turn off. I continued to go over and over in my head all of the things that need to be done. "I can't forget this, I can't forget that"...and add to that our church is making a pictorial directory which Loren insisted on us doing. As I laid there and thought about that I began thinking about how I didn't really want to do it. First of all, I don't like having pictures taken of me. YES, the queen of "selfies" does NOT like other people taking her picture! But also I was thinking about how much Loren has recently changed physically during his radiation treatment and chemo treatments. He has been on a huge amount of steroids and his face is very swollen. His hair has started to fall out again (we were told that would happen) and it is coming out in bald spots. I had already clipped it down really short last week, but I was laying there thinking that by the time he washes it in the morning it will probably be worse. I will probably have to shave it. Basically I was being selfish. I was thinking about how much time it would take do this, and there are so many other things I need to get done. I would wake up throughout the night still thinking about whether or not to go have our photo taken. By morning, as is often the case, God has given me peace and clarity. I need to look past my selfishness and realize that this is important to Loren. So we will. We will go to have our photo taken for the directory. I shaved his head this morning...and I will do the many other "things" on the list of "to do's" today. Among them sitting to do bills. My least favorite "chore" to do...isn't it everyone's? But reading Corinthians this morning it brought a new light to that for me. Our life has changed drastically financially in the last nine months, and most certainly since October when Loren moved into long-term disability. After reading Corinthians this morning I thought to myself how I have changed my outlook because of my trust in God on this matter. HE has taken care of us time and again through the love of HIS people and I have a deeper appreciation for EVERYTHING that Loren and I have. I honestly have to say that when "times were good" I am not sure that I truly appreciated everything that we had. Not that we ever lived "large" as people say nowadays, but what we did have I never stopped to look at it as a gift. My outlook now? It is ALL a gift! Everything we have, everything we are given is TRULY a GIFT! My "old" ways of thinking have been made "new" through this journey we have been on. Maybe not every moment of every day do I have this realization, but often, when I become the most distressed about "things" I am able to calm myself by remembering this.

Yesterday was day sixteen of twenty-three radiation treatments for Loren. Almost near the end of radiation treatments. He is really starting to feel the effects of the treatments now. Especially since they are beginning the weaning of the large amount of steroids he has been on. The radiologist told him yesterday that his fatigue will probably begin to be a lot worse. He is taking two naps a day now...long naps. Whatever it takes for his body to heal...whatever it takes. He has begun to have a strange gait...we noticed it yesterday after we came home. After treatment today we will come home so he can get a nap and then we will be going to have our photo done. Because he wants to....I love him dearly....pray without ceasing for us, because sometimes I'm just too tired to pray.

February 18, 2015

~ Okay family and friends, today I figured out that I was off on my count on the radiation treatments that Loren has had. Today was day number eighteen. His treatment time took longer today which was a bit disconcerting at first, but when the technician brought him out she explained why. He has five more treatments left. Today when they were doing his treatment they took many images. They are preparing him for what they call "boost" treatments. These next five treatments will have more intense radiation to a more targeted area.

He has tolerated his treatments very well but in the last week he has been very fatigued. He has had increased lightheadedness...which we are told is NOT attributed to the radiation (don't know if I'm buying that) but in any event he takes a couple of long naps a day which I am glad about. The more rest, the better. Asking for continued prayer that Loren will remain healthy and tolerate these last treatments well, and that God's healing hand be at work through the hands of the doctors he has placed in our lives. God bless.

February 19, 2015

~ Fatigue setting in...slept an hour through my alarm today. Loren and I are both fighting the overwhelming fatigue...

*****

~ For months Loren and I have believed that if it be God's will we will see the miracle of complete healing in Loren. Tonight I just read a post from a woman I have known for years. She was diagnosed years ago with MS. She has been through many things because of the illness including losing the sight in her left eye nine years ago. This morning after all these years she regained the sight in her eye! Praise God from whom all Blessings flow! Through HIM ALL THINGS ARE POSSIBLE! Loren and I have renewed HOPE that complete healing through HIM is absolutely possible! We will continue to believe that, understanding that it has to be HIS will. WE HAVE FAITH AND WE HAVE HOPE THAT MIRACLES CAN AND DO CONTINUE TO HAPPEN!

February 20, 2015

Jesus Calling ~
"Learn to live from your true Center in Me. I reside in the deepest depths of your being, in eternal union with your

178

spirit. It is at this deep level that My Peace reigns continually. You will not find lasting peace in the world around you, in circumstances, or in human relationships. The external world is always in flux—under the curse of death and decay. But there is a gold mine of Peace deep within you, waiting to be tapped. Take time to delve into the riches of My residing Presence. I want you to live increasingly from your real Center, where My Love has an eternal grip on you. I am Christ in you, the hope of Glory"

~ This morning after a time of anxiety and fear I said to Loren, "I just want peace, that's all I want, and I don't know if I will ever feel that in my life again". Between Loren's illness and a whole plethora of family issues my mind and my heart is in a constant state of racing thoughts and things, that while I know I have no control over them, they continue to take over my every thought. Preparing to leave for the day, I opened up Jesus Calling and read today's devotion...Dear God you are ALWAYS here and ALWAYS know what is in my heart...

February 22, 2015

~ As you might imagine, the word "heal" although only being four letters long has been an enormous word in my vocabulary for the past ten months. For some reason this morning the word "heal" has resonated in my head over and over again. Even as I sat in church and tried to concentrate on the words of the prayers and of the homily this word was there in the forefront...literally, over and over. I don't really need to look very far. Loren is always connected to that word along with a continual prayer in my heart and mind, "Father in Heaven, I KNOW, and WE KNOW if it be YOUR WILL that Loren WILL BE HEALED of his cancer." But truthfully, we are ALL in need of healing. Each of us has pain in our lives whether it is physical, emotional or spiritual. We all need to be healed. There has been far too much pain in my life in these past ten months. Just over ten months ago Loren was diagnosed with brain cancer. A pain which brought me to my knees. A pain that I wondered in the beginning how we could continue to move forward each day. My father's death in June and the pain that brings may never have a complete healing. The pain of hearing my mother share her grief on the other end of the phone when we speak. The pain my sister shares of her own grief about my father's death. I find myself wondering about how you begin to heal from all of this. Then there are the other experiences in your life, family issues of which our family has had far too many of in these last few months. How do you begin to heal these things? I don't know the answer to that. As this word "heal" has become a part of my being recently I have realized that there will be many things that may never have a resolution to them, so how do you "heal" from them? The last few days I have had an anger welling up in me. Yesterday I had tears of anger when my husband wanted to fix me a cup of coffee. A simple task which has become monumental for him. The tears and the anger just welled up inside. Anger because this was a man who could do most anything. I would mention something to him and he would find a way to do it, make it, or figure it out. Now everything is a task that takes so much time and effort. I am in need of my anger to be healed....for many reasons...spiritually being among them. I find even though I go to HIM for comfort and strength, I find myself being ANGRY with God! ANGRY that this would happen to my precious husband and that HE won't HEAL him NOW...if ever. I find myself wondering if it will be HIS will to heal Loren. So, I am need of healing spiritually as well. The exhaustion sets in and I'm too tired to pray, and I don't care because I am ANGRY at HIM! "Shepherd me oh God, beyond my wants, beyond my fears, from death into life." Yes, I need to be shepherded, beyond all my wants and fears and healed from all the pain and fear in our life. Is that possible? I'm not sure, but when I can pray...when I do pray, that will be my prayer. Not just for me, but for everyone who needs "healing" in whatever way you need it. For now, I ask that you continue to pray for Loren's complete healing and strength.

It's been a difficult day...can we just go back thirty-four years, start all over again and not have any idea of what lies ahead?...

February 24, 2015

~ Tomorrow will be Loren's final radiation treatment. Over the weekend Loren shared with me that he feels that this radiation is most definitely going to be the instrument that God is using to take away the lymphoma. This morning as I was getting myself ready for the day and to take him to his treatment the number "17" was resonating through my mind. As many of you know, the number "17" has deep meaning to my family. As I thought of the number "17" I was thinking of my Dad.

When I came downstairs I picked up my phone. Tomorrow's date is 2-25-2015...add those numbers together. That would be "17". My Dad's way of letting me know he is with us on this journey. "17"...I don't believe in coincidences....

February 25, 2015

1 Thessalonians 5:18
"In everything give thanks, for this is the will of God in Christ Jesus for you."

~ Today was the last of twenty-three radiation treatments for Loren! Praising God who brought Loren to this day! Loren said today while we celebrated afterward that while he has been on that table he "imagined a black hole being where the cancer has been." To which I responded, "...and I am imagining God's Grace and Light replacing that black hole!" Praying it is HIS will that this is so! RING THAT BELL HONEY! RING THAT BELL!

MARCH 2015

March 5, 2015

Hebrews 7:25
"Therefore He is able to save completely those who come to God through Him, because He always lives to intercede for them."

~ As we have done continually throughout these months we place ourselves before our God asking HIM to give us peace, comfort and strength.

We are at the cancer center this morning where they are preparing Loren for his infusion. Before his infusion he had to have some blood work done and saw the PA. Not the best news this morning. I've been concerned the last couple of days. Loren's coloring hasn't been very good. He is kind of pale, most especially his lips. Blood work shows all of his counts are down. He is once again neutropenic. They are also sending his blood work off for testing. They are concerned that lymphoma cells may be in the blood. We won't know the results of that for a week. They will be giving him IV antibiotics this morning as well. In the meantime he will have to come back at least a couple of times for injections for his white cell count and more blood work in a week. A gut punch. After twenty-three days of radiation we thought we might have a reprieve. Please continue to pray for Loren's strength and that he stay healthy. I am concerned as I have had a bad cough for the past week, praying it hasn't passed to him.

March 7, 2015

Psalm 63: 7-8
"For you have been my help, and in the shadow of your
wings I sing for joy. My soul clings to you, your right hand
upholds me."

~ We spent many hours awake through the night. (Far more than usual) Since Loren has been weaned off of his steroids the aches and pains of the neuropathy after having months of chemo are setting in. He has spent the last few days in a good bit of pain in his right shoulder. Every movement is excruciating for him. When discussing this with the doctor the other day we could come up with no clear way to treat it. We opted for the conservative way because Loren is on so many medications. Even after weaning him off of two medications recently he is still on many others and we didn't want to add a prescription pain killer to the mix. We chose to use ice and heat and take Tylenol Arthritis as it is stronger than regular Tylenol. He was in so much pain that around 3:30AM I wanted to put him in the car and take him to the ER even though his white cell count is down and that's probably the worst place he should be. He convinced me not to and said if he talks it helps to take his mind off of things. So, we laid in bed for the next two hours, discussing many things, until both of us grew tired enough to slip back to sleep. A couple of hours later he is awake and is in much pain again, but at least now we can get up, eat something and he can take his Tylenol. As he laid there thinking out loud he said, "I'm not sure what this is...is it the lymphoma?" I'm not going to let darkness take over this man's battle! Please pray with me for Loren, that God release him from this pain and that he start living that "quality of life" that Dr. Dunbar so often speaks about.

*****

~ It's been a rough couple of days...and then something happens and you realize that God once again is showing you HIS love through HIS people, and that HE knows what your concerns are and HE is walking this journey with you, hearing your every prayer. Loren has a friend he has known for a number of years. As he is a kind and humble man I know he would not want us to say who he is. Last weekend I spoke with him and asked him if he would help us with something. He didn't hesitate an instant, and today he called to say he had taken care of it for us. GOD IS GOOD! And because we "feel that not expressing gratitude when we are grateful is like wrapping a present and not giving it", we wanted to share how incredibly grateful, thankful and blessed we feel right now. Thank you to God and thank you to our friend who answered HIS call without hesitation!

March 8, 2015

1 Chronicles 16: 9-10
"Sing to Him, sing praises to Him; speak of all his wonders. Glory in His Holy name; let the heart of those who seek the Lord be glad."

~ Today God's Wonders include lessening the pain that Loren is feeling in his arm. Last night he was able to sleep a bit more comfortably than he was the night before, and for that we are singing HIS praises! Praying that as today continues that the pain will continue to lessen more. Another issue has cropped up since late last night. We are prayerful that Loren is not seeing the return of the C-diff bacterial infection that he had back in the fall. With his immune system being low that is definitely a concern. We are trying by all costs to avoid a trip to the emergency room this weekend. He will have an appointment at the oncologist's office tomorrow and that would be much better than having to be in the ER. Prayers for that to happen please.

*****

~ We didn't make it through the weekend. We spent most of today in the ER where they decided they needed to admit Loren to the hospital. His blood counts had dropped further so they have given him one unit of blood and are going to give him two more. The doctors will consult in the morning to decide whether or not to give Loren platelets as well. His pain in his shoulder continues, but at least here they can give him stronger pain medication. As always, Loren continues to have deep faith, strength and fight. I'm the one who doesn't. Asking prayers for Loren that the doctors will be able to figure out why he has pain so that they can relieve it permanently and that Loren's counts rebound faster than they have in the past. Please pray that I may have renewed strength and faith to continue this journey the way Loren deserves me to. God bless.

March 9, 2015

Galatians 5: 22-23
"But the fruit of the Spirit is love, joy peace, longsuffering,
kindness, goodness, faithfulness, gentleness, self-control.
Against such there is no law."

~ "Fruits of the Spirit"...spending time reading Jesus Calling today and Galatians 5:22-23 is one of the passages for today's devotion. Yeah, I would say that today I am missing A LOT of the fruit on my branches. Let's see, the "love" the "joy" the "peace" the 'kindness" the "goodness" the "gentleness" and the "self-control" all got lost along the way of advocating for my precious husband. As Dr. Dunbar likes to say, "The bull dog is in the building." A lot went into my losing the "fruits of the Spirit" today, but suffice it to say, I got my point across and it is clear that I expect NOTHING but the ABSOLUTE BEST CARE for my husband, whether I am in the room or not. And, I guess I don't feel too bad when my husband shared with me that the young man that came to take him for his MRI late this morning told him on the way downstairs, "You are so lucky to have someone like her looking after you." Deep breath...

So, the update is that there isn't much to update. Blood work from this morning shows Loren's white count up just a smidge...we'll take it. However, his platelets have dropped off even more and they will be giving him two bags of platelets. He has developed a rash around his trunk this afternoon. There are conflicting ideas of what it could be. One opinion is that it could be shingles, which if it is, they feel it is being suppressed by the fact that he has been taking Valtrex prophylactically for months now. The other opinion is that it is hemorrhaging under the skin from his platelets being so low. If it is low platelets their hope is the rash will rectify once Loren receives the platelets. If it's shingles other than continuing on Valtrex and pain meds which he is on for his shoulder there isn't much else to do. MRI results aren't back yet so nothing to report there. Continued love and prayers sent our way...strength and healing for Loren...and a bit of that "self-control", "kindness", "gentleness" etc. for me.

March 10, 2015

Psalm 46:5
"God is within her she shall not fail. God will help her at break of day."

As a very wise woman told me the other night, "one day at a time, just get through one day at a time". Thank you Mom, I love you, thank you... ~ "At break of day"...

March 13, 2015

John 16: 33
"I have said these things to you, that in Me you may have peace. In the world you will have tribulation. But take heart; I have overcome the world."

Jesus Calling ~
"Learn to live above your circumstances. This requires focused time with Me, the One who overcame the world. Trouble and distress are woven into the very fabric of this perishing world. Only My Life in you can empower you to face this endless flow of problems with good cheer.
As you sit quietly in My Presence, I shine Peace into your troubled mind and heart. Little by little, you are freed from earthly shackles and lifted up above your circumstances. You gain My perspective on your life, enabling you to distinguish between what is important and what is not. Rest in My Presence, receiving Joy that no one can take away from you."

~ Oh, as usual, how very appropriate Jesus Calling is for us today. "Learn to live above your circumstances". Dear God how I wish I could stay focused on you at this time. I must confess, nothing, absolutely nothing that I have experienced up to this point in our lives, could have prepared me for the "trouble and distress that has been woven into the fabric of our life". Nothing physical, nothing emotional, nothing spiritual. I never saw myself here in this place. The pain of this journey with all of its twists and turns, not just with Loren's illness but with family issues, has me wondering often how we go on.

I never considered that I would be reaching with outstretched arms EVERY moment of EVERY day for the peace, the strength, the comfort that only HE can give. We all should, but in the "busyness" (is that a word?) of every day, sometimes we forget that HE is there in every moment of our day and we should speak to HIM regularly throughout it. I haven't until now. Sometimes it is within my own head and sometimes it is a guttural "DEAR GOD IN HEAVEN". It escapes my mouth each time my body strains to be here to give my husband strength...physical strength to move from one point to the other throughout his day. It escapes my mouth as I lay down at night praying that HE give us both the rest we need to restore our bodies and our souls.

It has been a difficult week. Loren went into the ER on Sunday. His counts had dropped off critically and he is having horrendous pain. No Tylenol, no pain killers, no muscle relaxants seem to make a difference. It is a strange pain. One where one moment it is there and the next he has absolutely no pain. The hospital discharged Loren on Wednesday evening. I wasn't comfortable with the decision. I'm still not. He cannot get anywhere in our home without assistance. I am thankful to our daughter-in-law once again for having shown me the mechanics of being able to help him. Although it does take a toll on my fifty-four year old body. Yet my "Dear God in Heaven" at those moments when I call upon HIM gives me the strength I need to help Loren. Wednesday night there was no sleep for either of us because of Loren's pain. On Thursday morning at 8:00 I was on the phone with our insurance company to see if we needed a referral for physical therapy. We got an appointment for 2:30 yesterday afternoon. It is clear that the therapist was not really sure what to do, although he has ordered therapy for Loren. He also prescribed a new medication for Loren. Not quite sure what it was supposed to do, but what it did do was make him go to the bathroom literally EVERY hour for the first four hours of going to bed last night and every other hour thereafter. It was one more night with no sleep for either of us because physically Loren is not able to get up and down to use the bathroom himself.

Next week Loren's oncologist will be back in the office (he is on vacation this week). At that time we are hoping to learn the results of the blood work that was sent off last week. There are some other things that have been discussed with us that will probably have to happen in the near future. Once we are clear on those facts I will share them with you. In the meantime we ask that you continue to pray for us. Strength, comfort, and peace and that God in his infinite mercy relieve Loren of his pain. God bless.

March 15, 2015

~ Once more we come to you family and friends and ask for you to lift us up in prayer. Loren is once again in the hospital. His pain in his shoulder has increased and he now has pain in his lower back and none of the pain medication seems to be helping it. It takes the edge off but doesn't relieve it totally. Today was so very difficult. I had finally reached a point because of how weak he was feeling that I literally could not move him from one place to another in the house. I had to call our son and daughter-in-law to come and help and it took the two of them to do it even with our daughter-in-law's skills as a PTA. It was so disheartening to me that we had come to a point that I could no longer do what Loren needed me to do to help him physically.   Not just disheartening, it was devastating. It was a difficult decision to bring him back to the hospital, especially to bring him to Atlanta as it is just so much more convenient to have him in Fayetteville, but we have not been at all pleased with the care he receives while he is there. So far his blood work has come back "pretty good for him" as the ER doctor said. Still anemic and platelets are still low, but his white count did improve. He has developed another issue. He can't seem to pass urine. He keeps feeling as if he has to but then barely does. They did a scan and his bladder is full. They have opted to not 'cath' him at this time because they don't want to cause any other issues because of his immune system being compromised but that is still on the table. Some more news that has hit hard is that the CT scan they did has the radiologist concerned with what he has seen. Tomorrow they have a brain MRI planned as well as a spine MRI. Our journey seems to have taken a turn in a different direction. Prayers for strength, peace and comfort as we continue on.

*****

~ Everyday holds the possibility of a miracle...and until God shows us HIS plan in this journey we will hold onto this hope.

*****

~ As has been the case on many occasions God once again today showed me HE is here with us, loving us through HIS people. I received a text earlier today from a precious friend of mine who I have come to know in the past couple of years. Through this time she has shown me time and again what a beautiful spirit and woman of faith that she is. She has the rare ability to look right into your soul and she listens to it, really listens to it...not just with her ears but with her heart which is truly a rare gift. She apparently was not going to take "no" for an answer when she said she wanted to come up to Atlanta and "give me a hug". When she arrived I went downstairs to meet her and the first thing I did was apologize to her because I was quite the sight. Her response... "I love it." I love her. We went down to the cafe where she treated me to something to eat, but more importantly she listened. Truly listened with a heart that has been blessed with that rare ability I spoke of. As I began to ramble she just looked at me with her beautiful eyes and just listened. Uninterrupted she let me go on and on. Her eyes filling with tears as tears poured from mine. I don't know how long I spat out my words of pain and fear but she just patiently listened. When I finally was spent with emotion she looked at me and said, "God touched my heart this morning and I knew that this was what I was sent to do today." God loving us through HIS people. HE sent me one of HIS beautiful servants today to show me HIS presence here with us as we continue this journey. It brought me such peace and helped release me of anxiety and fear. I had no doubt of HIS presence in that hour or so that I spent away from my husband and HIS eyes shone brightly through hers.

March 17, 2015

John 5: 11-13
"This is the testimony: that God has given us eternal life,
and this life is in His Son. He who has the Son has life; he
who does not have the Son of God does not have life.
These things I have written to you who believe in the
name of the Son of God, that you may know that you have
eternal life, and that you may continue to believe in the
name of the Son of God."

~ ...and it is our belief in God The Father, God The Son and God The Holy Spirit Who have cradled us in THEIR arms and carried us along this journey and have brought us to this place.

Today we are so grateful and feel so much love in our hearts for every one of you who have covered us with your love and support from the moment we began this journey nearly a year ago.

Yesterday Loren spent four hours having MRI's done of his brain and his spine. Last night Dr. Dunbar called with the news that the lymphoma is now in the spine.

In my heart I expected this news. This morning Dr. Dunbar came to our room. She spent a good bit of time discussing the findings and that they would like to begin radiation to alleviate the pain that Loren is feeling. When she finished the "medical" discussion she turned to Loren and said, "Loren, we have come to a place where we will not be able to treat the lymphoma any longer." The entire conversation I watched Loren's face. He laid there quietly looking at her, nodding from time to time. She glanced over at me, then back to Loren. She asked him, "Do you understand what I am saying to you?" He nodded to her and said, "Yes, I understand". She began to cry and looked at him and said, "You are an amazing man." Yes, this I have known for more than half my life. I won't share anymore of the conversation but I will tell you that it is "in the knowing that there is peace". Strange, but very true. We are not denying that there will not be anger and sorrow as Loren continues his journey. The journey that he has prayed himself to his entire life and most especially this past eleven months, the journey to our Heavenly Father, if it was not to be HIS will that Loren be cured of his cancer. We ask now more than ever that you pray us through this time. Prayers of peace, comfort and strength for the both of us and for our family. We are so very thankful for each of you. Our hearts are so full of love for you all.

March 19, 2015

~ For nearly a year I have written time and again about Loren's brothers...his "Delta Family". This afternoon his supervisor came to the hospital to visit Loren and to once again gift us with their amazing generosity. While we sat talking he said, "I have something to show you." He opened his phone and showed us a picture. We couldn't believe our eyes. It was a picture taken at the fundraiser held in Loren's name that morning. There was a line of Loren's "Delta Family" as far as you could see. This "family" gathered in Loren's name today to show us how much he is loved and cared about as they have so many times throughout this journey. There were not enough words to share with

Loren's supervisor how much they have meant to us during all of this. They have continued to call, email, Facebook and come by to see Loren. Some of them even leaving work to get him and bring him for lunch and then sit and visit with him when they brought him home. It warmed my heart to hear Loren share time and again his conversations with his "family" and see that smile on his face that he has been so well known for all of his life. He reminded a few of us the other night that in his yearbook he had been voted "best smile". I love this man. When his supervisor left and I shared the beautiful card from them and the contents it brought tears to his eyes and he said, "I'm just so sad that I will never be able to repay them for all that they have done for us. You know, all those years that I would buy those biscuits and things I never realized what a difference it was making in someone's life...until now." Our hearts once again are so full of gratitude to all of you and yes, Loren is right, we will never be able to repay you for all you have done for us. God Bless each and every one of you.

March 21, 2015

~ Yesterday was a difficult day. But what a blessing it was for me that my sister arrived in Atlanta very early in the morning. She was by my side while Loren had a very uncomfortable morning and we spent several hours together trying to get him as comfortable as possible. Fortunately, they seem to have found the combination of pain medication that relieves most of his discomfort and by afternoon we sat together in his room and watched him get much needed sleep. In between that time there were many phone calls that needed to be made. Frustrating calls...calls that I should not have to make because for months I have been trying to get the answers that I absolutely MUST have now. There were many tears of frustration and anger and sorrow and my sister was beside me through all of them. How is it that I am the "big sister", but she seems far more capable, and far stronger than me? She let me cry and made me laugh even through the sadness and frustrations. I wish she could stay here forever as we walk towards the part of this journey we prayed we would never come to. But, I am glad that at this time she is here to lift me up through the turmoil and sadness that is our life right now. I love you Sue.

*****

~ Loren was surprised by his lifelong buddy Mike who came into town and walked into his hospital room this morning. You often read about friends that you don't see very often but how that special bond remains and is renewed in just a few minutes time. It has always been the case with these two. It warms my heart.

March 22, 2015

John 11: 41-44
"So Jesus, perturbed again, came to the tomb. It was a cave, and a stone lay across it. .Jesus said, "Take away the stone. "Martha, the dead man's sister, said to him, "Lord, by now there will be a stench. He has been dead for four days. "Jesus said to her, "Did I not tell you that if you believe you will see the glory of God? "So they took away the stone. And Jesus raised his eyes and said, "Father, I

thank you for hearing me. I know that you always hear
me, but because of the crowd here I have said this, that
they may believe that you sent me." And when he had said
this, He cried out in a loud voice, "Lazarus, come out!" The
dead man came out, tied hand and foot with burial bands,
and his face was wrapped in a cloth. So Jesus said to them,
"Untie him and let him go".

~ The word of God touches each of us and speaks to us in different ways. I'm certain, like me, you each have a favorite passage or gospel reading. John 11: 1-44 has always been that one for me for two reasons. "Jesus wept"...showing us that HE was truly "God made man", that HE shared all of the emotions that we do, of the depths of sorrow at losing someone we love, and because HE so loved his friend Lazarus that HE performed the ultimate miracle of bringing a dead man back to life. For me this gospel reading has always told me that in whatever situation we are experiencing in life there is always hope. In our present circumstances my hope and comfort is in knowing that Loren believes to the depth of his soul that God The Son is "the resurrection and the life. "He who believes in Me, though he may die, he shall live. And whoever lives and believes in Me shall never die." Loren has lived his life accordingly. I will keep these words in my heart through every moment of every day that goes by.

*****

Psalm 61: 2
"When my heart is overwhelmed, lead me to the ROCK
that is higher than I."

~ ...a message from my mother today.

March 24, 2015

Isaiah 41: 13
"For I, the Lord your God, will hold your right hand,
saying to you, fear not, I will help you."
Jesus Calling
"This is a time in your life when you must learn to let go:
of loved ones, of possessions, of control. In order to let go
of something that is precious to you, you need to rest in
My Presence, where you are complete. Take time to bask
in the Light of My Love. As you relax more and more, your
grasping hand gradually opens up, releasing your prized
possession into My care.
You can feel secure, even in the midst of cataclysmic
changes, through awareness of My continual Presence.
The One who never leaves you is the same One who never
changes: I am the same yesterday, today, and forever. As
you release more and more things into My care,
remember that I never let go of your hand. Herein lies
your security, which no one and no circumstance can take
from you."

~ I'm not going to lie. As the days continue to pass I
have found it harder to feel God's hand in mine as this
journey goes on. But I know HE'S there. HE knows I know
HE is there and HE knows what my heart is feeling.

The past several days have been filled with so much emotion. Happiness that my sister and Loren's best friend were here to spend time with Loren and with me. My sister has a way of bringing laughter to even the most difficult of situations and an inner strength and support that I was blessed to have in those few days. Pain, anger and fear are inevitable when one is experiencing losing a loved one, but this journey has been made worse by the incompetence of people who should be on top of their game in reference to what their job entails. Fortunately for us Loren's supervisors have compassion for what we are experiencing.

But, yesterday afternoon I reached out to the woman who was so very helpful to me at the beginning of this journey and was reminded once again of what a woman of faith she is. She has called periodically throughout this year to check on Loren, but to also make sure I was doing alright. It is not her job to walk with me at this point, but she did not hesitate when I called her. She advised me to "sit tight" until she got back to me and before we hung up she said, "I am not going to hang up this phone until I hear you breathe...take a deep breath and let it out, and know that I am on this for you." God holding out HIS right hand to me letting me know HE is here with me.

It did Loren good to spend time with his best friend Mike for a few days. Their connection still after all these years runs so deep and I was sad that Mike had to leave...as well as my sister. She was my anchor, keeping me calm and grounded when my emotions wanted to take over.

Loren's pain continues to be managed fairly well. He had a good bit of pain through the night but finally around 2:30AM they had given him enough pain medication that he was able to get comfortable enough to sleep for several hours.

His appetite has been going back and forth between being ravenous and not really wanting to eat...he just has to have the right thing! He's had this habit of ordering the same thing for breakfast, lunch and dinner, but how many PB&J sandwiches can you eat?! So yesterday on my way back from running some errands I brought him back a Wendy's burger. Oh yeah! He scarfed that baby down! I'm thinking that was some good medicine!

He continues to lay quietly throughout the day in prayer. His faith in God never wavering. I am reminded daily of how I have never felt the same strength in my faith as he has shown me our entire life together. I ask for your continued prayers of peace, comfort and strength. Love to you all.

*****

~ It puts a smile on my face to know that Loren's "Delta Family" continues to not only keep him in thought and prayer, but continues to come and spend time with him, letting him know that he matters to them and that they will walk this journey along with him. Loren's friend, one of his Delta brothers, stopped to get him Chinese food for lunch to which Loren said, "Well, I'll eat a little, but I'm not very hungry"...and then, like his Wendy's burger, scarfed a good bit down. Then this evening I was finally able to meet his friend from Delta who is one of the guys who has been instrumental in the incredible generosity shown time and again to us from Loren's "Delta family". Such a great guy, and in minutes I felt like I'd known him as long as Loren has.

March 26, 2014

~ Today was a day I had hoped would never come. A day when the realization of Loren's diagnosis a year ago would be leading in a direction I had hoped this journey would not go. Even now as I sit and write this I am not allowing my mind to fully grasp it. I close my eyes and I wonder over and over again, did I not pray hard enough, and was my faith not deep enough? And then I realize that God has a plan for each of us. A plan for Loren and a plan for me, and a plan for each of you. We know now what God's plan is for Loren, we do not know the timing, but we know the plan. God intends to bring Loren home. To welcome Loren into HIS Heavenly home. How can something so incredibly beautiful bring such sorrow to us? Perhaps it is just the fear that we don't know what God's plan is for us, and in my case, I don't understand HIS plan for me. Loren and I were finally in a place in our lives where we were enjoying the "fruits of his labor" all of these years. We would sit quietly in our home and look around and say, "We so love our home, we so love our life together." We would enjoy a long weekend away here and there with no worries or cares because our family was grown and on their own. Why God? Why now? Why must this be your plan now? We will never know the answer I suppose until we meet our Heavenly Father.

Until then I will ask HIM to help me understand HIS plan, help me to understand.

Today Loren went to hospice...the part of this journey we had hoped we would never have to make. Tonight I am full of sorrow. I had expected to be able to stay with him. I will not be doing that...rules. Nearly every hospital stay I would stay with him, most of the time. To know that I will come home every evening leaving him there is heartbreaking to me. I'm not sure I will ever get used to that. So once again my friends and family, I ask you to pray for Loren and for me. Prayers of comfort, strength and peace as we continue on this journey. God bless.

March 27, 2015

Philippians 4: 19
"But my God shall supply all your need according to His riches in glory by Christ Jesus."

~ Another day of holding onto hope. The hope that we can only find in our Lord. My hope is that HE knows, although I am struggling, that I truly trust in HIM and have faith that HE will guide my heart and my mind through this path that HE has both Loren and me on. It is hard, but HE is there.

My heavy heart was eased this morning when the first words from Loren's mouth to me after "good morning" were "they take such good care of me here", and then "you made the right decision Libby. They showered me this morning and when I was trying to get back into bed I almost went to the floor, but they caught me. You wouldn't have been able to do that." Although I am saddened with how weak Loren's body has become I am happy that he realizes that the need for him being in hospice is one that was best for his safety and well-being. It is still difficult for me, but he seems more at peace with it and so I am.

I don't know why I am amazed at how God continues to show me HIS love through HIS people, but I continue to be. On my way home this evening a received a phone call from a precious friend of mine. She shared some beautiful things that are being done for Loren and me and my heart is full of love for all of my incredible "family". I do not have enough words that describe what this phenomenal group of people has meant to me and to Loren all of these months. That is not said with exaggeration, it is the truth. They have smothered me with love, prayers and support day in and day out for all of these months and I know that I can rely on them to love us through this journey.

God is taking care of our every need even though I am finding it difficult to surrender myself to HIM. Praying my heart will continue to be open enough to recognize HIM showing me HIS love through HIS people. God Bless.

March 29, 2015

~ It has been several days with family coming into town to spend precious, tender moments with Loren.

Last night we said goodbye to our children and grandchildren. Not knowing God's plan from one day to the next...one moment to the next is difficult. It's been a difficult day already and it isn't quite 9AM. This morning

I said goodbye to Loren's family. It was a beautiful few days just spent around Loren. Loving him through this journey. None of us wants to be here, but it is the walk God has placed before all of us. I don't know how to do this. But I suppose no one really does. I want to spend every moment there with him, but I know I can't. "Life" gets in the way. There are "things" that have to be done...at home; errands to be run and the nuns who run the hospice have established "rules" that keep me from being with him at night. That is the worst. I had become accustomed to spending the times he was in the hospital with him, most of the time. Apparently the "rules" are there to protect me from overload I suppose, but it's not helpful even though I know why. The nights are the hardest. Even though I slept last night every dream was overtaken by this journey. Strange dreams but when I would wake up it was always Loren there in the dream just before waking which never made sense when I would recollect the dream. Getting ready to do some things that need to be done and then to spend the day with Loren. I'm never certain what he will be like when I arrive. Yesterday was not a good day when I got there. He was in a lot of pain.

I'm praying his night and his morning are better today. Asking continued prayers for understanding, peace, comfort and strength.   God Bless.

*****

Ecclesiastes 3: 1
"There is a time for everything, and a season for every activity under heaven."

Jesus Calling ~
"Stop trying to work things out before their times have come. Accept the limitations of living one day at a time. When something comes to your attention, ask Me whether or not it is part of today's agenda. If it isn't, release it into My care and go on about today's duties. When you follow this practice, there will be a beautiful simplicity about your life: a time for everything, and everything in its time.
A life lived close to Me is not complicated or cluttered. When your focus is on My Presence, many things that once troubled you lose their power over you. Though the world around you is messy and confusing, remember that I have overcome the world. I have told you these things, so that in Me you may have Peace."

~ Oh Dear Lord, why do I continue to be amazed at our Father in Heaven? HE knows every thought, every fear, every sorrow...HE knows it all! Today's Jesus Calling says everything! I've been spending SO much time trying to "work things out". My humanness is keeping me from fully believing that God is walking beside me in this journey. HE IS ALREADY THERE! HE knows what will come. I must start believing that "HE has plans to prosper me and not harm me." Oh to be able to completely surrender to that. My heart I am certain would be far less heavy. I am sitting here watching Loren sleep. He is comfortable and seems peaceful. I wonder "where" he is...from time to time he clasps his hands in what seems a prayerful state and even reaches up at times. I know that even in sleep he continues to prepare himself to meet his

Heavenly Father. Praying my faith remains through this journey.

March 30, 2014

~ Today Loren will be retired from Delta Air Lines just shy of his 34th year with them. Through the years there have been many changes at Delta and the airline industry as a whole, but one thing never changed for Loren, and that was his loyalty to them. He raised his family and provided a wonderful home and life thanks to Delta. In October we had a discussion as to whether or not Loren should retire or move into long-term disability. He wouldn't hear of retiring. He never lost hope that he would return to Delta. I recalled this morning his exact words as we discussed it. "I want to leave Delta on my own terms." As we have realized throughout this journey, life is not on "our terms." God's plan is not always what our life plan is. Loren will retire from Delta today like he has lived his life, without "fanfare", without attention. He has never been an attention seeker. He is a humble, quiet, simple man who lived his life that way. Our heartfelt thanks to Delta Air Lines. While we've never "lived large", we always have had a comfort in our lives that we know not everyone can say they have had. Most of all, thank you to Loren's immediate "Delta Family". You have helped us through this journey this past year in more ways than we can count and we are so grateful to you all. God Bless.

March 31, 2015

~ So what was that I was saying yesterday about Loren retiring with "no fanfare" Ha! His "Delta Family" was apparently not going to let that happen! This morning I received a text from Loren's supervisor who said that he and about eleven or twelve guys had a cake and wanted to come by and celebrate Loren's retirement with him! What can I even say? There are no words to describe what I feel in my heart for all of these guys. You know, the ones "who would never even know I was gone" as Loren had once told me. This "family" has nonstop let us know that Loren is missed and that, as we like to say at Spring Hill Elementary, "You matter." They walked in the door one after another shaking Loren's hand congratulating him on a job well done and there were even a few "Loren stories" shared. My heart is full of love and gratitude to all of these men who, since day one, have been there for us. There is a Delta slogan "One great airline"...yes it is, but these guys, the ones no one sees out front are the heart and soul of Delta Air Lines. They are what make it "great". Thank you to each and every one of you for making Loren feel that "he matters"...today and every day! God Bless!

APRIL 2015

April 1, 2015

~ My brother Pete and my sister-in-law Robin have been visiting us for the past couple of days. They are a couple of worker bees and are doing the things at our home that have been sorely neglected in this past year. I love them so much for all they have done but most importantly for all the emotional support they have given me these past couple of days. As Pete said he "didn't want to come." He is still riding the emotional rollercoaster of our Dad's death and he did not want to face that with Loren. I am thankful he did. Feeling very blessed to have them both here...even though they are outside at the crack of dawn working!

*****

"Pain and suffering have come into your life, but remember, pain, sorrow, suffering are but the kiss of Jesus ~ a sign that you have come so close to Him that He can kiss you." ~ Mother Teresa

~ Asking for prayers for Loren. I have watched him these past few hours and he is in so much pain. Since I arrived here today they have given him pain medication three times, but there seems to be no relief in sight. Please lift him up in prayer that God releases him from this pain. Thank you.

＊＊＊＊＊

~ Precious moments with family...and many friends who have come by the hospice today. So thankful for these many gifts God has given us in our lives. My brother reminded me today as we left the hospice, "Elizabeth these are good people you have in your life, really good people." He is so right.

April 2, 2015

~ Last night was a night of tossing and turning and very little sleep. Every thought was consumed with Loren after the day he had yesterday. With each day that goes by the realism of where this journey is leading becomes irrefutable and the "things" that consume my day are compounded in emotion by the fact that I want ALL of those "things" to just go away! It's so unfair that I should have to, that ANYONE should have to deal with these "things" in the face of a journey like this in their life. But there is no choice.

However, the real reason for this post today as I get ready to start the day with the myriad of "things" to deal with before going to sit by Loren's side is how my head and my heart are full of "GRATITUDE" this morning. My thoughts have been filled with ALL of you. I know with all of my heart that there is absolutely NO way we would have made it through this journey without ALL of you by our side. The prayers, the visits, the many ways you have helped us. We have gathered strength from all of it. Strength, peace and comfort have blanketed us throughout this entire journey. So, since waking this morning and preparing to start the day I want ALL of you to know that you are in my heart, in my every thought and every prayer. "May you wake with GRATITUDE"...I know I did, did you? Take a moment...you may not be experiencing a journey similar to ours, but take a moment, breathe and thank God for the many things in your life you are grateful for. God bless.

*****

~ Thanking you all this evening for your prayers for Loren yesterday. Today was a much better day for him. He never really complained today at all about pain, just a little discomfort. Praise God! This afternoon his nurse Joseph and assistant Peter actually moved him into a recliner. He took a good nap there and then ate his dinner sitting up in the chair and was quite talkative. When they helped him back to bed I sat a long time quietly next to him watching him sleep. Every once in a while he would open his eyes and say, "Oh good, you're still here." Throughout the day he would occasionally say something odd. We've come to expect that. I was thinking that perhaps it was all the pain medication, but when I spoke with the doctor today he said that he didn't think so, that it was more likely the disease progressing. I left a bit earlier tonight as I had received a message on my phone of thunderstorm warnings and didn't want to take the chance of driving on the freeway during it. (We all know how much I love freeway driving!) As I was leaving and giving Loren his hugs and kisses for the night he said, "Just like Little House on the Prairie, huh?" I asked him, "How so?" He said, "You know, this log cabin, it's just like

211

"Little House on the Prairie." ~ "Yes honey, it is. It's just like that." It was a good day. God bless.

April 3, 2015

~ Holy Week has always been precious to Loren. One year ago Holy Saturday was Loren's diagnosis of brain cancer. Throughout this past year Loren spoke often of having missed Holy Week and Easter last year. Yesterday our dear friend and pastor, Father John, came to visit Loren. I was in another room with the social worker. My phone rang...it was Loren. He hasn't been calling me on the phone. That is a difficult task now for him to figure out. "Hi honey, are you all right?" "Yes, I need you to bring me some clothes." "Okay, why do you need some clothes?" "Well, Father John is here and we are going to go to Mass." After Father John left Loren continued to talk about going to Mass. His faith continues to be the center of his life, even though he is now finding it more difficult to pray. I am certain that he is standing close to his Redeemer at this time. I asked him yesterday if he had "talked to Jesus today?" He said, "Yes, not for very long, but I did." "Oh, I'm glad honey, I'm sure HE is still here listening." "Yes, HE is".... Let us all remember today that Jesus hung upon that cross to be our Redeemer, so that as we lay "talking" to HIM we can have the confidence that HE IS STILL HERE LISTENING TO US as we prepare to take HIS hand and he leads us to our Heavenly Father.

*****

~ It's a beautiful Good Friday afternoon in Atlanta. One of our son's came to visit and we all went for a walk on the beautiful grounds of the hospice. Praising God for this glorious day and the time to spend together.

April 4, 2015

Psalm 23
"The Lord is my Shepherd"...

Jesus Calling ~
"I meet you in the stillness of your soul. It is there that I seek to commune with you. A person who is open to My Presence is exceedingly precious to Me. My eyes search to and fro throughout the earth, looking for one whose heart is seeking Me. I see you trying to find Me; our mutual search results in joyful fulfillment.
Stillness of soul is increasingly rare in this world addicted to speed and noise. I am pleased with your desire to create a quiet space where you and I can meet. Don't be discouraged by the difficulty of achieving this goal. I monitor all your efforts and am blessed by each of your attempts to seek My Face."

~ Loren's heart has sought our Lord each and every day of his life. Through this journey he has set his eyes on HIM to give him strength, courage and most of all peace. He has had a "stillness of soul" that I don't understand. I have stood beside him for the past thirty-four years and I cannot understand how a human being can have such "stillness of soul". Through this journey I have never once heard him cry out in anger. We have talked of his sadness of not being here for his grandchildren, but never anger. Neither have I seen him have fear. He has expressed fear for me. Not wanting to leave me alone, but I have assured him time and again, I won't be alone. I will have all of you and I will have our Lord, with a renewed relationship with HIM. One that has grown throughout this journey. And, I will have him watching over me. I will not be alone.

Psalm 23 ... Loren has prayed this psalm over and over again in this past year. "Even though I walk through the valley of the shadow of death, I will fear no evil, for YOU are with me, YOUR rod and YOUR staff, they comfort me"... Our Lord has accompanied us on this journey and HE has comforted us, most certainly Loren.

Tonight one of the nuns, the charge nurse, says she will do her best to bring Loren's bed to the chapel so that he can celebrate Easter Vigil fulfilling Loren's longing to do so since last year. And, I will be watching his face throughout; knowing his heart and soul will be full of the peace that only our Lord can give. God bless each and every one of you and may the peace of Christ be with you at this Easter and always.

*****

~ ...Shaking his head..."No, I'm not today" Loren says with his eyes closed...I have no doubt he is speaking to our Lord. I am certain Loren is standing close to HIM at this moment....be still my heart...

*****

~ Sister has agreed to bring Loren to the chapel tonight to celebrate the Easter Vigil. In an hour from now Loren will be doing what he has spoken about for an entire year...celebrating the miracle of Easter. Praising God for this blessing today.

*****

~ What a beautiful celebration of our Lord's resurrection. I wish you all had been here with us. Moving Loren to the chapel he became a bit agitated and uncomfortable. But as soon as he began to hear the litany and smell the incense he became peaceful. Later in the Mass when the chaplain at the hospice began the blessing of the baptismal water I turned to look at Loren. Dear God I wish you could have seen the smile on his face. When I turned back to Father he was looking at him too. He nodded at me and we both smiled. During the consecration I turned again to look at Loren and he had a tear coming down his face. It was all I could do to keep from falling apart. Giving thanks tonight for celebrating our Risen Lord with my husband and for the peace that HE placed in Loren's mind and body this evening. I will not forget this night.

April 5, 2015

Psalm 4: 8
"I will lie down and sleep in peace, for you alone, O Lord, make me dwell in safety."

~ This morning I arrived at the hospice to find Loren quietly resting. The staff said that he had had a peaceful night. He has grown more tired and weak. He has talked to me this morning but has not opened his eyes. He knows he is weak, he tells me he is. Throughout the day and night God has heard and answered my prayers of peace for Loren. I don't want him to have another day like he had yesterday. Our Easter miracle...peace...Yesterday I received several phone calls and texts from family and friends wanting to FaceTime with Loren. Please know that it was his decision not to do so, and I am respecting those wishes. I am certain that will be his wish again today. Continue to send messages and texts to him. I will read them all to him. God bless you all, a beautiful Easter to you and may it be full of God's promise of peace for us all.

April 6, 2015

"Life is a balance of holding on and letting go" ~ Rumi

April 7, 2015

~ This morning as I have been preparing to spend the day with Loren my mind is swirling with thoughts of his day yesterday and wondering how I will find him today when I arrive. Yesterday was a difficult day. He was very restless. From the moment I arrived he wanted me to "help him with his barbells"...he had been "working out". Those of you that know Loren well know that he has always taken good care of himself. He was an athlete growing up in Minnesota, and all of his life he watched what he ate (most of the time) and worked out. His motto was, "I eat to live, not live to eat." He wasn't a workout fanatic, just enough to stay fit and strong. When his health started to fail last year it was difficult for him because he was too tired and weak to work out. I think this need to be "working out" now is his mind being so aware of the weakness in his body. Praying today will be a more peaceful day for him.

My thoughts were also full of the words "happiness" and "contentment." The past year in our lives has been full of sadness and difficulties. Without going into details, suffice it to say, that "family" has not been what it should be in times like this. It is only by faith and daily prayer that strength to get through each day happens. I started to think this morning about those two words "happiness" and "contentment" and realized that there are so few people who in their lives "feel" them...truly "feel" them. I have no doubt Loren has. His deep faith, first and foremost is the reason, but also because Loren has never wanted to "control" anything or anyone in his life. Every day we go through our lives wanting to control situations around us, or people in our lives, whether it is family or friends or co-workers. It doesn't work. All it does is bring us unhappiness. Sure, we like to blame our unhappiness on others, but the unhappiness is really ours alone. Loren has always been content to sit quietly and observe. He never found the need to have control in any way. Some find that weakness, but the gentle, quiet contentment is who he is.

Recently we were having a conversation with one of our children. I asked the question, "Do you think that for the past thirty-four years there haven't been times that I haven't been unhappy? Because if I told you I wasn't I would be lying. If anyone tells you that they are lying." Loren sat by quietly listening and then said, "I was never unhappy." I turned and looked at him. Dear Lord, in thirty-four years this man was NEVER unhappy? Proof that once again, as I have said many times in the past thirty-four years, if I had been married to anyone else I would have been divorced three times over. Somehow, I believe him. Somehow I know that my life has been blessed by the most extraordinary man. A man like few others, that because his faith in knowing that his happiness and contentment was not to be found in "things" or in the "control" of others. "Control" only destroys and causes pain, of that I am sure. I've seen it with my own eyes; I'm seeing it now in present circumstances in our life.

Praying today that we all might realize that there is only ONE in control. When we surrender to that I am sure that we all might find that "happiness and contentment" in our lives. Loren did, and has continued to surrender himself to the ONE who is in control. That is why throughout this entire journey I have never seen him angry. Complete surrender to Divine Providence.

Shame on me for only "recognizing and appreciating what I have" now. Stop now and take a moment to recognize and appreciate what you have. Remembering that we are not in control and we never know when all that we have and all that we hold dear will be taken away from us...

April 8, 2015

Matthew 11: 28-29
"Come to me all who are weary and burdened, and I will give you rest, I am gentle and humble in heart, and you will find rest for your soul."

*****

John 2:25
"And this is the promise which He Himself made to us:
Eternal Life."

~ Today God's promise to us all was fulfilled for Loren. I have written many times in the past year about Loren and the way that he had lived his life so that the promise of Eternal Life would be his. Of this I have no doubt. Loren passed peacefully this afternoon surrounded by family and friends and the prayers of so many who have loved us through this journey. He died just as he had lived; with a contentment and peacefulness that few of us know in our lives. For some time our hearts will be full of sorrow at the loss of this precious man, but we know that today he heard the words of our Heavenly Father, "Welcome HOME good and faithful servant, welcome HOME."

I cannot express enough thanks and gratitude to all of you, our family and friends, who have loved and prayed us through this journey. I ask that you continue to do so, because now begins the real heartache in that we now have to learn to live our lives without this beautiful, humble, peaceful man. I had not intended to journal this evening, but my heart is so full of love for all of you that have sent me messages this evening that I felt the need to share with all of you ~ his journey is complete. God Bless you all.

April 9, 2015

Exodus 33:14
"My presence shall go with you, and I shall give you rest."

~ I have been sitting quietly this morning, reflecting on each moment of the day yesterday and holding Loren close to my heart. I reached for Jesus Calling as I have nearly every morning since receiving it as a gift months ago. As always, the words are speaking directly to me. Exodus 33:14 is one of the passages for today's reading. "The Lord replied, "My Presence will go with you, and I will give you rest."... My heart is full of the joy that I know Loren felt and is feeling now as I am certain those are the words he heard from our Lord and Savior. "Do not be afraid Loren, My Presence will go with you, and I will give you rest." Much needed rest after a long journey. God is good.

I called the office of Loren's neuro-oncologist Dr. Dunbar today to tell her that Loren had passed away yesterday. She was with patients but called me at the end of the day. When I answered the phone her voice quivered and before I could get a word out she said, "Libby I have to tell you something. For the past three nights I have dreamt of Loren and I knew that he was making his transition." And this is why we loved this doctor so. She is so spiritually connected to her patients and such a woman of deep faith that she is able to know where her patients are in their journey...this woman is nothing short of amazing.

April 11, 2015

Romans 12: 12
"Rejoice in hope, be patient in tribulation, be constant in prayer."

~ This morning I have been laying here with Loren close in mind and heart. I have been thinking of a conversation that I had numerous times throughout this year, but most especially in these last few weeks. When I would share with people how Loren and I would talk about his feelings and emotions about this long journey. I would say, "He's never been angry, never." I know that they would look at me and wonder how that was possible. After all, we are often told that "anger" is one of the "stages" people go through during a serious illness and in grief. I certainly had my moments of anger, and when I did Loren and I would talk about it. But, he was never angry...sad, but never angry. He would talk about his sadness of possibly leaving me and his children and grandchildren, but never angry. Romans 12:12. "REJOICE in hope...this incredible man NEVER lost hope. He ALWAYS hoped that he would be healed, that he would return to work and our life would be what we had always hoped it would be at this time. . However, only IF it were God's will to do so. He ALWAYS had hope. "Be PATIENT in tribulation." I'm not sure if there were another human being more patient than my husband. Good Lord! He was married to me for more than thirty-four years! I mean come on! How much more patient would a man have to be?! But seriously, his patience throughout his illness was astounding. He would talk often about his lack of ability to do the things that he would like to be able to do, but his physical body just would not allow him to do it, but through it all he never lost patience...or hope. He would say, "When I start feeling better I'm going to get myself back in shape"...I would always nod my head in agreement. He was always patient while he was undergoing treatment. ALWAYS the nursing staff would talk about how kind and patient he was to all of them. He was a favorite. Often there would be disappointment when one or the other of them was not assigned to be his nurse. "Be CONSTANT in prayer."...ALWAYS, he was ALWAYS in prayer. So many times I would look over at him and he would have his eyes closed, and I would ALWAYS ask the same question, "Are you alright honey?" It was ALWAYS the same answer, "yes, I'm just praying." Just praying...just praying. CONSTANT in prayer. We were married thirty-four years and I would say that I learned more from this man in the past twelve months than I have in more than half my life. Dr. Dunbar told Loren the day she shared with us that there was no more treatment for his illness that he was "an amazing man." If she only knew. She truly only had an inkling. Just an inkling. I pray that the lessons I have learned from Loren in this past year will remain with me for the rest of my life, however long that may be. Holding you close to my heart my precious husband.

April 15, 2015

~ One week ago today around this time I was sitting quietly next to the man I have spent more than half my life with. He had gone "HOME" to his Heavenly Father and I was just sitting there watching him. I'm not sure if I was expecting something to happen or not. There was a lot of activity in the room. A lot of conversation and a lot of phone calls being made. I wish now that I had not made phone calls at that time. I wish that I had respected the sacredness of that moment. I think about it now and realize that I will never have that time back. Kind of like now. The busyness of this past week has left little time to reflect on the journey in those final hours and minutes on that last day. I was so afraid as we moved closer in those last days of going on that journey with Loren. But I had told him that I would be okay and that when God stretched out his hands to him that I wanted him to go with HIM. That I knew that he had prayed himself to that moment and that he shouldn't hesitate to go. He promised me that he would. I sang and hummed "On Eagles Wings" to Loren in those last couple of hours and minutes with him and I know that God is "holding him in the palm of HIS hands." It brings me peace to know that. Such sacred time, that we were privileged to have been able to share with him. I am blessed.

April 18, 2015

Ephesians 4: 2
"Be completely humble and gentle; be patient, bearing with one another in love, Make every effort to keep the unity of the Spirit through the bond of peace."

~ This was Loren to the very core of his being. This was who he was, no pretense involved. Yesterday as we came together to celebrate Loren's life it became so crystal clear to me that the man I knew Loren to be was who he had been his entire life. A gentle, kind, quiet strength, and a man of deep faith. So many of us try throughout our lives to "reinvent" ourselves. Never being content with who we are. Not Loren. Conversation after conversation with people who had known Loren for years and years, from childhood friends to co-workers of more than twenty-five years, I heard the same thing over and over again. "Loren was the best guy." "He was a humble guy." He was a man constant in his demeanor and his beliefs. A man who was so humble that he had often said to me, "no one will ever notice when I am gone."

Dear God, I don't even know where to begin. Yesterday was Loren's "funeral", but it quickly became apparent that this day was not going to be a day of sorrow. It was going to be a day of remembering a man who was extraordinary... but not because he did extraordinary things. It was because he was being remembered as a man who because of his kindness, because of his quiet strength and because of his faith had touched so many lives. He never realized it, but oh how it was shown yesterday. Our family received the most amazing blessing yesterday by the friends and family that came to celebrate Loren's life. Utter amazement at the sea of blue...our Delta "family" was there in full force. I was speechless. I was overwhelmed with emotion at the outpouring of love and respect for Loren from his "family". Time after time I was told of how special Loren was by so many of these men. Blown away, simply blown away.

One of his nurses from the hospital in Atlanta where he began his cancer treatment was there. I was so touched. She was one of the extraordinary nurses who cared for him time and again when he underwent treatment. I couldn't help but share with everyone how special she was.

The service itself was absolutely beautiful. I know Loren was pleased. We were blessed to have Father John a longtime friend and our pastor to celebrate the service and who gave such a moving and very personal homily. The chaplain at the hospice and several of our deacons were also there. The choir was made up of members from many of our churches choirs and they sang so beautifully. I tried so hard to "stay present" throughout the service. It was difficult at times, but I did find myself thinking that this did not seem sorrowful, that it was supposed to be a celebration and it felt like that. Wonderful readings, beautiful music and heartfelt words. Loren's best friend Mike gave the eulogy. There couldn't have been a better choice. As I told him, probably no one knew him better...not even me.

As I sit here and write this it is quiet and still in the house. It is the first time in days that I am alone... really alone. There is a loneliness that I am feeling, but it also feels good to sit and reflect on everything that has happened in the past week. To be alone with my thoughts and feelings. Looking at pictures, old and new, of Loren's smiling face it is making it hard to fathom that he is gone. That the familiar things, the "constant" things will no longer be each day. Many people have said to me in the past few days, "you're doing so well" and I would respond with "yes, I am, I am at peace." I am, for the time being. I know that this new "normal" will be difficult to adjust to, but I promised Loren I would be okay, and I plan to keep that promise. I thank you ALL from the bottom of my heart for the incredible showing of love, support and prayers that you showered upon me and our family yesterday. I will not forget it. God Bless.

April 19, 2015

~ So often during this past year Loren and I would talk about how we didn't know what changes lay ahead for us, but that we would continue the journey together for however long it took.

One year ago today Loren and I received news that would drop us to our knees and change our lives...forever, but he NEVER gave up hope, NEVER!

Would God restore Loren to health here on earth or would he be restored to health only when he journeyed HOME to HIM? We now know it was God's will to bring Loren HOME to HIM. I can only imagine the joy that Loren is experiencing now. As Father John said during his beautiful homily on Friday, when he was talking to Loren he said, "No one really knows what Heaven is like." No, no we don't. We can only imagine. My imagination is one of joy, beauty and a body that knows no limitations. Glorious, only glorious.

Now, with Loren gone, I can't even begin to imagine what God has planned for my journey. I never saw myself here. Never saw myself without my wonderful husband. Not now, not at my age. But, I suppose one never does. I look around my world. I know many women who are walking this same journey. Courageous, wonderful women. My mother, Loren's mother, his sister and so many others.   I am watching them. I want to walk this journey like them. I want to be courageous like them. I want to keep that promise I made to Loren numerous times throughout our journey together; that I would be okay. When my sister left yesterday morning she hugged me and she told me that she was so proud of me. She told me that she had watched me grow in so many ways in this past year, and that she was proud of who I have become.   I've thought a lot about that good-bye yesterday. I've thought about how that's what life is about, isn't it? It's about looking into the face of our challenges and our pain and growing from them. Not being crushed by them. Realizing that although we may not want to travel in the direction of the journey God has placed in front of us, but that there is always the chance to grow if we walk faithfully in that direction. Moving forward I have the gift of knowing that my life has been blessed by the most extraordinary man. I am choosing not to think of him as having been taken away from me far too soon, but rather that God brought Loren, HIS good and faithful servant, HOME to HIM and that he is being rewarded because of his faithful life to HIM. It is the only way I feel I will be able to not become angry and bitter. I don't want to live my life that way. My journey is not over... I don't know where it will lead me, but it is not over. I want to follow Loren's example. I want to be a "good and faithful servant". My journey continues...

MAY 2015

May 1, 2015

Jesus Calling ~
"You are on the path of My choosing. There is no
randomness about your life. Here and Now comprise the
coordinates of your daily life. Most people let their
moments slip through their fingers, half-lived. They avoid
the present by worrying about the future or longing for a
better time and place. They forget that they are creatures
who are subject to the limitations of time and space. They
forget their Creator, who walks with them only in the
present.
Every moment is alive with My glorious Presence, to those
whose hearts are intimately connected with Mine. As you
give yourself more and more to a life of constant
communion with Me, you will find that you simply have
no time for worry. Thus, you are freed to let My Spirit
direct your steps, enabling you to walk along the path of
Peace."

~ Today's devotion does a much better job at explaining what I am feeling. This passage; "There is no randomness about your life" says everything to me. I don't understand why Loren and I experienced what we did and why I am experiencing this journey in my life now..."lean not on your own understanding"...but it is most obvious to me that I am on "a path of HIS choosing." I am trying my best to remember that HE walks with me in this present journey and I am trying my best to stay in the present by not worrying about the future...HE is

229

already there. I am doing my best to allow HIS Spirit to direct my steps. I am allowing myself to mourn when those moments hit me, but I choose to find the joy in each day. HE wants me to, and I know Loren does as well. As Loren said just weeks before he passed, "I was always happy." Yes, he was, he chose to be, and so will I.

There has been no randomness to the experiences throughout my life and most especially in this past year. My journey continues, and I will be obedient to HIM...

~ONE YEAR LATER~

More than a year has passed since my beloved left his physical body and went "HOME." Since that time I have been asked on numerous occasions how I have been able to be "at peace" with that. Truthfully, I am not always. It is easy to sit and think about how this was supposed to be "our time." The time in our lives when, with the children grown and gone, we were to have been experiencing a new chapter. When I spend time "there" in those thoughts it would be easy to become angry and bitter. But when your faith in HIM tells you

"To everything there is a season, and a time to every purpose under heaven" (ECC 3:1),

and you allow both your heart and your mind to grasp that truth then it is easier to find that peace.

In the beginning of the journey of grief and mourning after Loren's death I walked around in a fog. I look at that fog now as a "veil" of protection. People would tell me I was "numb" and I would be offended. Truly, how could one be "numb" after experiencing what I had? But I realize now that they were right. If I were to have fully grasped ALL of the pain of Loren's death after the year of his illness and all that needed to be done legally, financially and emotionally, I am certain that it would have been extremely detrimental to me. And so, God in HIS infinite mercy protects us with HIS loving "veil." And then, as time goes by, the veil begins to lift. You begin to realize that this is your new life. It doesn't feel "new." With "new" you should feel excited. You should feel refreshed and renewed. You should have "joy" in this "new" life. Not so in the "new" that is experienced after the death of someone you love. Your "new" is fraught with pain and fear and exhaustion and loneliness and a depth of sorrow that you have never felt before. But you begin to learn to put one foot in front of the other each day. You hold on to the faith that carried you through those dark days when you hear those words one would never want to hear. "Your loved one has cancer." And somedays your hands ache with the pain of clutching onto HIM with a strength you never knew you possessed. Because to let go would mean that you give up. I WILL not give up. I WILL continue to hold on to the faith that brought us through the year of Loren's illness and the faith that has brought me through this past year since Loren's death. And I hear HIM so clearly now as I did through all that time,

"For I know the plans I have for you," declares the Lord, "plans to prosper you and not to harm you, plans to give you hope and a future." Jeremiah 29:11

As I continue on this journey those are the words I will cling to, every morning and every night. I will believe them with my whole heart and soul and I will look forward to what HE has planned for me even on the days it is the most difficult to walk through the door and into the life HE has given me.

In God's eyes, in HIS perfect vision of Loren's life, Loren had completed his purpose here while in his physical body. I know I cannot be certain of ALL that God's purpose was for Loren, but without a doubt I know one of his purposes. It was to love me. To love me with a quiet, peaceful and unconditional love. His purpose was also to show me that I am far more capable, far stronger and able to do more in this life than I ever believed I could. Through the journey of Loren's illness and the year since his death I have begun to believe that. It is hard for me to wrap my head around the fact that he had to endure all that he did and to leave his physical body in order for me to learn these things. But he did. And I am. I am still learning so many lessons about myself. Loren's purpose continues…even after his death. I have to believe this, because if I do not than everything Loren and I experienced in our last year together and everything I have experienced in this life since his death is wasted. There is beauty to be found even in the sorrow and pain.

Our life's experiences are many and varied, but one thing I know for sure. They are NOT random. Embrace each experience whether joyful or painful. Learn from them. Most of all, be grateful for them and know that HE walks beside us along each one of them. God bless.

CPSIA information can be obtained
at www.ICGtesting.com
Printed in the USA
LVOW10s1822290117

522527LV00015B/590/P